T0328479

Cambridge Elements ≡

Elements in Corporate Governance
edited by
Thomas Clarke
UTS Business School, University of Technology Sydney

CORPORATE GOVERNANCE

A Survey

Thomas Clarke
University of Technology Sydney

CAMBRIDGE
UNIVERSITY PRESS

CAMBRIDGE
UNIVERSITY PRESS

University Printing House, Cambridge CB2 8BS, United Kingdom

One Liberty Plaza, 20th Floor, New York, NY 10006, USA

477 Williamstown Road, Port Melbourne, VIC 3207, Australia

314–321, 3rd Floor, Plot 3, Splendor Forum, Jasola District Centre,
New Delhi – 110025, India

79 Anson Road, #06–04/06, Singapore 079906

Cambridge University Press is part of the University of Cambridge.

It furthers the University's mission by disseminating knowledge in the pursuit of education, learning, and research at the highest international levels of excellence.

www.cambridge.org
Information on this title: www.cambridge.org/9781108964029
DOI: 10.1017/9781108966719

First published 2021

A catalogue record for this publication is available from the British Library.

ISBN 978-1-108-96402-9 Paperback
ISSN 2515-7175 (online)
ISSN 2515-7167 (print)

Corporate Governance

A Survey

Elements in Corporate Governance

DOI: 10.1017/9781108966719
First published online: January 2021

Thomas Clarke
University of Technology Sydney
Author for correspondence: Thomas Clarke, t.clarke@uts.edu.au

Abstract: The recognition of the profound impact of corporations on the economies and societies of all countries of the world has focused attention on the growing importance of corporate governance. There is an ongoing diversity of corporate governance systems, based on historical cultural and institutional differences that involve different approaches to the values and objectives of business activity. Sound corporate governance is universally recognized as essential to market integrity and efficiency, providing a vital underpinning for financial stability and economic growth. As the adequacy of the existing dominant paradigms of corporate governance is increasingly challenged, the search for coherent new paradigms is a vital task for corporate governance in the future.

Keywords: Corporate Governance, Boards, Directors, Shareholders, Stakeholders, Corporate Responsibility, Paradigms

ISBNs: 9781108964029 (PB), 9781108966719 (OC)
ISSNs: 2515-7175 (online), 2515-7167 (print)

Contents

1 Introduction

Corporate governance is of critical importance in a global economy where corporations are the leading players. Corporations have assumed the role of the compelling force in the transformation of the world economy, 'the engine, worldwide, for private sector participation in the global market – to raise capital, create jobs, earn profits, and divide the value added among those contributing to its success' (OECD 1998: 13). The ownership and control of corporations, the purposes they pursue, and the ways they are controlled will determine the prospects for economic and social stability (Clarke, O'Brien, & Kelley 2019).

1.1 Defining Corporate Governance

The recognition of the profound impact of corporations on the economies and societies of all countries of the world has focused attention on the growing importance of corporate governance (Clarke 2017). The most generic definition of this concern is that '[c]orporate governance is the system by which companies are directed and controlled' (Cadbury Report 2002: 15). Among the competing definitions of corporate governance, Margaret Blair's estimation encompasses 'the whole set of legal, cultural, and institutional arrangements that determine what publicly traded corporations can do, who controls them, how that control is exercised, and how the risks and returns from the activities they undertake are allocated' (Blair 1995: 3). In a similar vein Davis (2005: 143), in *New Directions for Corporate Governance*, suggests corporate governance refers to 'the structures, processes, and institutions within and around organizations that allocate power and resource control among participants'.

However, selective interpretations of the definition and purpose of corporate governance abound, and at one extreme this is reduced to: 'Corporate governance deals with the ways in which suppliers of finance to corporations assure themselves of getting a return on their investment' (Shleifer & Vishny 1997: 737). The OECD proposed a broader and more responsible definition and purpose of corporate governance when it first published the original *OECD Principles of Corporate Governance*:

> A good corporate governance regime helps to assure that corporations use their capital efficiently. Good corporate governance helps, too, to ensure that corporations take into account the interests of a wide range of constituencies, as well as of the communities in which they operate, and that their boards are accountable to the company and to the shareholders. This, in turn, helps to assure that corporations operate for the benefit of society as a whole. It helps to maintain the confidence of investors – both foreign and domestic – and to attract more 'patient' long term capital. (OECD 1999: 7)

More expansively still, Cadbury (2000) in work for the World Bank idealistically recognized the role of corporate governance in contributing to the stability and equity of society and the economy: 'Corporate governance is concerned with holding the balance between economic and social goals and between individual and communal goals. The governance framework is there to encourage the efficient use of resources and equally to require accountability and stewardship of those resources. The aim is to align as nearly as possible the interests of individuals, corporations, and society'.

Therefore, the definition and meaning of corporate governance varies considerably according to the values, institutions, culture, and objectives pursued: 'Corporate governance may be defined broadly as the study of power and influence over decision-making within the corporation . . . . Existing definitions of corporate governance are closely tied to different paradigms or ways of conceptualizing the organization or firm' (Aguilera and Jackson 2010: 5).

1.2 Diversity in Corporate Governance Systems

The expansive dimensions of corporate governance were narrowly translated in recent decades with the increasing ascendancy of financial markets and intellectual domination of agency theory into an almost obsessive concern for the problems of accountability and control involved in the dispersal of ownership of large listed corporations, and a rigid focus on the mechanisms that orientate managers towards delivering shareholder value (Dore 2000; Davis 2005; Clarke 2016b).

This Anglo-American hegemonic view of the purpose of the corporation and the direction of governance institutions has proved central to the progress of globalization, and the advance of international capital markets. The rather different cultural orientations of enterprise towards the economy and society in Europe, Asia, and other parts of the world have progressively been weakened (Clarke & Bostock 1994; Aguilera & Jackson 2003 and 2010; Clarke 2013 and 2017; Clarke & Chanlat 2009; Aglietta & Rebérioux 2005; Amable 2003). Both European and Asian perceptions of the role and significance of governance have changed in recent decades towards the Anglo-American view, in some respects simply in terms of formally adopting governance codes, in other ways more substantially such as in becoming more dependent upon Western capital markets. However, business leaders, governments, and regulators in Europe and Asia, while acknowledging the increasing salience of shareholder value, continue to recognize the substance of stakeholder values.

The insistent focus of corporate governance on boards, CEOs, and shareholders – oriented single-mindedly towards financial markets and shareholder primacy – has not served the discipline well. This approach not only narrows the dimensions of corporate governance to a restricted set of interests, but as a result it has a very limited view of the dilemmas involved in corporate governance (Deakin 2005; Clarke 2013 and 2014a). 'Bibliometric analysis of more than 1,000 publications shows that corporate governance research is characterized by both the use of agency theory as the dominant theoretical lens, and empirical samples from one country, typically the US and to a less extent the UK' (Kumar & Zattoni 2015a: 1; Durisin & Puzone 2009). In fact, there are continuing and competing corporate governance systems in the market-based Anglo-American system; the European relationship-based system; and the relationship-based system of the Asia Pacific, together with new approaches to governance in emerging economies. This ongoing diversity of corporate governance systems is based on historical cultural and institutional differences that involve different approaches to the values and objectives of business activity (Aguilera & Jackson 2003 and 2010; Aglietta & Rebérioux 2005; Clarke 2017).

Ignoring the possibility of different responsibilities and purposes for the corporation, the Business Roundtable of the United States, which represents the majority of the major US corporations, maintained a single-minded commitment to shareholder primacy from the issue of its *Principles of Corporate Governance* in 1997. In a sudden apparent abandonment of the doctrine of shareholder primacy at the Business Roundtable August 2019 meeting in Washington DC, 181 CEOs signed a new *Statement on the Purpose of a Corporation* (2019) committing to lead their companies for the benefit of all stakeholders – customers, employees, suppliers, communities, and shareholders. The substance of these wider commitments, beyond their symbolic value, will be revealed over time.

2 The Significance of Corporate Governance

2.1 The Origins of the Corporation

The first corporations were founded by religious and educational organizations, traders, and merchant venturers licenced by the state. The Dutch East India Company and the English East India Company were prominent examples of the great ambition and huge risk associated with early corporate enterprise (Frentrop 2019; Stern 2019). The 1844 Joint-Stock Companies Act in England facilitated the process of incorporation, and joint-stock companies quickly proliferated. Beginning in Europe and North America, but spreading eventually to almost all jurisdictions, some legal version of the corporation developed. The process of incorporation involves the abstract concept of clothing the entity with the 'veil' of juridical personality.

The conception of the corporation proved the inspiration for the modern business enterprise: the specific legal form of people and resources chartered by the state for the purpose of engaging in business activity. Unique characteristics distinguish the corporation from the other main legal forms – the sole proprietorship and the partnership. The vital elements of the corporation are:

- Limited Liability
  The losses an investor may bear are limited to the capital invested in the enterprise and do not extend to personal assets.
- Transferability of Shares
  Shareholder rights may be transferred without constituting legal reorganization of the enterprise.
- Juridical Personality
  The corporation itself becomes a fictive person, a legal entity which may sue or be sued, make contracts, and hold property.
- Indefinite Duration
  The life of the corporation may extend beyond the participation of its original founders (and may continue indefinitely).

2.2 The Increasing Scale and Impact of Corporations

As the scale and activity of corporations has increased immeasurably, the governance of these entities has assumed considerable importance. The corporation remains one of the most significant if contested innovations in human history (Coase 1937; Schumpeter 1942; Polyani 1941; Clarke, O'Brien, & O'Kelley 2019). 'It is not exaggeration to suggest that, with the possible exception of political democracy, the corporation has contributed more to human welfare than any other Western institution' (Stout 2019: 224). While the continuing influence of the state may have been neglected in global commentary in recent decades, the scale and influence of global corporations undoubtedly continues to grow and be recognized, even as their composition, structure, and operations are transformed. The largest international corporations have much greater economic clout than most countries in the world: if companies' revenues and selected emerging markets GDPs are compared, the leading one hundred corporations are much richer than most countries. The economies of most developing countries are diminutive compared to the revenues and assets of the largest international corporations. If we compare government total revenues with corporate turnover, of the world's largest 100 economies 31 are countries and 69 are corporations (World Bank 2016). And, of course, there are a lot more corporations: there are perhaps 200 viable countries in the world, versus several thousand large international corporations.

Though the number of listed corporations in the United States peaked in the 1990s and then began a precipitous decline with the bursting of the internet bubble and the concentration of the banks, the market capitalization of US listed corporations continued to grow exponentially, with the global domination of the US platform technology corporations (Apple, Amazon, Microsoft, Google, Facebook) (Clarke & Boersma 2019; Clarke 2019b). In the rest of the world there was a sustained increase in the number of listed corporations, with the total of global listed corporations increasing from 15,000 in 1975 to around 45,000 in 2015 (Figure 1).

Business corporations have an enduring impact upon societies and economies. '[H]ow corporations are *governed* – their ownership and control, the objectives they pursue, the rights they respect, the responsibilities they recognize, and how they distribute the value they create – has become a matter of the greatest significance, not simply for their directors and shareholders, but for the wider communities they serve' (Clarke & dela Rama 2006: xix). These concerns originated with industrial capitalism and have become accentuated with the extensive internationalization of corporate activity in recent decades, the global deregulation of financial markets, and a growing awareness of the damaging economic and social consequences when corporate governance failures occur.

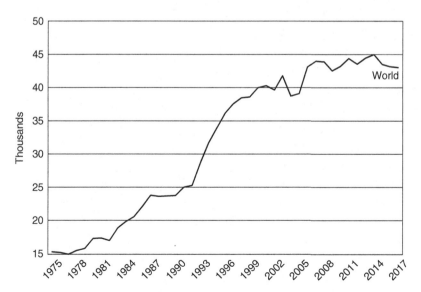

Figure 1 Increase in the number of global listed domestic companies 1975–2016

Source: World Bank (2018) https://data.worldbank.org/indicator/CM.MKT.LDOM.NO

Among governments throughout the world, sound corporate governance is universally recognized as essential to market integrity and efficiency, providing a vital underpinning for financial stability and economic growth. The leading international agencies including the G20, OECD, IMF, and World Bank have seized upon corporate governance as a means of managing the risk of recurring corporate failure, but also as a route to improving economic performance, facilitating access to capital, reducing market volatility, and enhancing the investment climate. This was formally acknowledged when the OECD *Principles of Corporate Governance* became the G20/OECD *Principles* in 2015, with the diffusion of corporate governance codes around the world (Cuomo et al. 2016).

2.3 The Theoretical Understanding of Corporate Governance

The subject of corporate governance has long held a fascination for economists, lawyers, and management theorists from the moral economy of Adam Smith (1759; 1776) to the present day. The frequent dilemmas involved in business formation and operation were highlighted by historians, who have noted the association of pioneering business activity in the first years of mercantilism and industrialism in the seventeenth and eighteenth centuries with fraud and corruption (Frentrop 2003 and 2019; Stern 2019). Early in the twentieth century, Berle and Means (1933) in response to the devastation of the Wall Street crash and Great Depression critically analyzed the strengths and weaknesses of the emerging modern corporation.

According to Berle and Means, professional managers were in a position to determine the direction of the enterprise, and shareholders had 'surrendered a set of definite rights for a set of indefinite expectations' (Berle & Means 1933: 244). After the New Deal reconstruction of the US economy and the end of the Second World War, many US corporations in the 1950s and 1960s grew massively in scale and market domination, achieving pre-eminent positions in world markets. A new managerial and corporate mode of coordination of enterprise based on organization and planning had arrived as analyzed by Coase (1937) and later by Chandler (1977), transcending the market. This was an era celebrated in Galbraith's *New Industrial State* (1967) in which corporate growth and brand prestige apparently had displaced profit maximization as the ultimate goals of technocratic managers, as planning and administration in close cooperation with government had displaced market relations as the primary corporate dynamic (Henwood 1998: 259). In this technocratic milieu a shareholder was 'passive and functionless, remarkable only in his capacity to share without effort or even without appreciable risk, the gains from growth by which the technostructure measures its success' (Galbraith 1967: 356). However, the Galbraithian idyll began to disintegrate with the severe recession of 1973–5, the incapacity of US corporations to compete effectively with Japanese and European products in key consumer market sectors on quality and price, and the push towards conglomerate formation by Wall Street, which was interested in managing multiple businesses by a new discipline of strict financial performance. Technocratic managerialism, focused on products and consumers, was forcefully displaced by financial engineering focused on market indices and financial returns.

At this insecure juncture in the US economy, a group of Chicago-based economists left an indelible intellectual impression of the agency problems of corporate governance (Jensen & Meckling 1976; Fama 1980; Fama & Jensen 1983). This focused almost exclusively upon the problem of principals (owners of shareholdings) ensuring their interests were pursued by their agents (the managers of the companies in which they held shares). This starkly simple proposition exercised a fierce grip on the understanding and analysis of corporate and managerial behaviour for many decades to come, and in turn this promoted the shareholder primacy movement which insisted that the duty of corporations is to deliver shareholder value above all other considerations.

This stripped-down principal/agency theory view narrows the dimensions of corporate governance to a restricted set of privileged interests, and as a result it has a very limited conception of the dilemmas involved in corporate governance: 'Our perspective on corporate governance is a straightforward agency perspective, sometimes referred to as separation of ownership and control. We want to know how investors get the managers to give them back their money' (Shleifer & Vishny 1996).

In reality, multiple theoretical and methodological perspectives are required for an adequate understanding of the complexities of corporate governance (Zattoni & Van Ees 2012; Filatotchev & Wright 2017). Each of the theoretical perspectives including agency, transaction costs, stewardship, resource dependency, stakeholder, managerial hegemony, and class hegemony have a different view on enterprise and governance, different disciplinary foundations, different problem focus, and different assumptions on organization and relationships.

Theoretical approaches to corporate governance follow a continuum from the narrow focus of agency theory and transaction cost theory inspired by financial economics, through approaches including stewardship, resource dependency, stakeholder, and managerialist theories developed by organizational theorists, to more critical analysis originating in sociological and political critiques with an expansive view of the whole political economy. (Clarke 2004a). Each theoretical approach has its own logic and limitations, and though a number of the approaches represent opposing interpretations of the same problem, in some cases the theories serve to illuminate different dimensions of the governance problem.

After agency theory, the most established theoretical approach is transaction cost economics. Ronald Coase (1937) insisted (notwithstanding the assumption of neoclassical theory that the allocation of resources is coordinated through a series of exchange transactions on the market) that in the real world a considerable proportion of economic activity is organized in firms. Coase examines the economic explanation for the existence of firms, and why economic activities take place within firms rather than through markets. He explains the nature of firms in terms of the imperfections of markets, and in terms of the transaction costs of market exchange.

New institutional economics differs from agency theory in that the corporate governance problems of firms are perceived to proceed from a number of contractual hazards. This approach is concerned with discovering internal measures and mechanisms which reduce costs associated with contractual hazards to an efficient level: the external discipline of the market cannot be relied on to mitigate these problems, as it has only 'limited constitutional powers to conduct audits and has limited access to the firm's incentive and resource allocation machinery' (Williamson 1975: 143). Like neoclassical economics though, the locus of attention remains the shareholder-manager relationship, but in this case it is because shareholders are perceived to 'face a diffuse but significant risk of expropriation because the assets in question are numerous and ill-defined, and cannot be protected in a well-focused, transaction specific way' (Williamson 1985: 1210; Learmount 2002). As with agency theory, the narrowness of the focus limits the explanatory power of this analysis.

In contrast to agency theory, stewardship theory acknowledges a larger range of human motives of managers including orientations towards achievement, altruism, and the commitment to meaningful work (Hernandez 2008 and 2012). Stewardship theory maintains there is no inherent conflict of interest between managers and owners, and that optimal; governance structures allow coordination of the enterprise to be achieved most effectively. Managers should be authorized to act since, according to stewardship theory, they are not opportunistic agents but good stewards who will act in the best interests of owners. Stewardship theory recognizes a strong relationship between managers' pursuit of the objectives of the enterprise, the owners' satisfaction, and other participants in the enterprise reward. Davis, Schoorman, and Donaldson (1997) suggest that as managers maximize shareholders' wealth through raising the performance of the firm, they serve their own purposes. Managers balance competing shareholder and stakeholder objectives, making decisions in the best interests of all. However, there is an element of choice in corporate governance arrangements. Both managers and owners can choose to have either agency or steward relationships, contingent upon their assessment of the motivations of each other, and the situation of the enterprise. Stewardship theory rescues the integrity of management as a profession, something many managers would recognize and aspire towards.

There is a stream of theoretical approaches that widen the focus beyond internal monitoring, to explore the external challenges of corporate governance in terms of building relationships and securing resources. Resource dependence theory, institutional theory, and network theory all are interested in the external relations of corporations. Resource dependency theory highlights the interdependencies of organizations rather than viewing them simply in terms of management intentions. Hillman, Cannella, and Paetzold (2000), for example, examine how company directors may serve to connect the firm with external resources that help to overcome uncertainty, and provide access to relationships with suppliers, buyers, public policy makers, and other social groups. Resource dependency approaches add a vital external dimension to corporate governance relationships. Stakeholder theory defines organizations as multilateral agreements between the enterprise and its multiple stakeholders. The relationship between the company and its internal stakeholders (employees, managers, owners) is framed by formal and informal rules developed through the history of the relationship. This institutional setting constrains and creates the strategic possibilities for the company (Blair 1995; Clarke 1998). While management may receive finance from shareholders, they depend upon employees to fulfil the productive goals, to innovate, and to develop viable purposes and strategic intentions for the company. External stakeholders (customers, suppliers, competitors, special interest groups, and the community) are equally important, and also are constrained by formal and informal rules and interests that businesses must respect. Stakeholder theory has an intellectual appeal and practical application to the complexity of business enterprise, however it is argued from an agency perspective that multiple stakeholder responsibilities can leave management with too much freedom of maneuver, substituting their own interests for the shareholder interests (or even wider company interests).

From a more critical perspective, managerialist theory focuses on the distinctions between the myth and the reality of the relative powers of managers and boards. Mace (1971), for example, examines the 1960s ascendancy of US corporate executives, when powerful CEOs selected and controlled the boards of directors of the companies they ran. He outlines how CEOs in the US were able to determine board membership, decide what boards could and could not do, control the information and professional advice the board received, and determine the compensation of senior executives, including often themselves. When corporations fail, the question always arises, 'Where were the board of directors?' However, there is a wide gap between what directors are supposed to do, what people generally assume directors do, and what they are actually allowed to do in practice, or are inclined to do. Mace catalogues how dysfunctional boards, rather than being exceptional, became normal in the United States, as executives took control.

Finally, there are more radical theoretical critiques which suggest that corporations perpetuate the power of an elite, serving to exploit others in the interests of accumulating wealth and power for a few privileged shareholders and executives (Mills 1971). Though radical analysis faded after the 1960s, it has enjoyed a new lease of life in the widespread critique of the impact of globalization which corporations have spearheaded, with unemployment in developed countries and poor working conditions and pay in emerging economies where multinational corporation investment is concentrated. Most recently, there is a radical critique of the sustainability of corporations, that questions the impact of industry on climate change and the damaging impact on the ecology (Bansal and Hoffman 2011; Clarke 2016a and 2019; Helm 2015; IPCC 2014; Stern 2006).

In conclusion, the almost exclusive focus on agency theory in recent decades in the attempt to understand corporate governance has limited the field of inquiry, and the conception of shareholder value as the single defining corporate objective has fatally narrowed perceptions of corporate purpose and performance. The shareholder value regime is deeply flawed in terms of an understanding of directors' duties (Blair 2012), company law and practice (Deakin 2005), and executive incentives (Lazonick 2012), and conveys a lack of understanding of, or interest in, what actually takes place in companies in terms of the advance of innovation or the generation of wealth (Lazonick 2010 and 2017).

2.4 Accountability and Strategic Direction

Boards of directors acting solely as monitors for shareholders, as envisaged by agency theory, is a one-dimensional view of the role and responsibilities of directors (Blair & Stout 2001). The sad paradox of this exclusive focus on the monitoring of company directors to ensure they deliver shareholder value is that this excludes full consideration of the value-creating role of boards (Huse 2018). Boards of directors have a vital role to play working with the executives in leadership of the company and in value creation. This role is often neglected because of the emphasis of regulation upon the control and accountability functions of the board, and because of the almost exclusive focus of agency theory on control and monitoring. Corporate governance is not simply about accountability. Governance has an important role to play in value creation, innovation, and strategy (Huse & Gabrielsson 2012; Zattoni & Pugliese 2012). Governance without strategy leads to paralysis, as strategy without governance leads to recklessness.

Yet as international corporate governance regulation developed, and codes were formulated with corporate governance thrust into prominence by high-profile company failures, the concept of corporate governance almost universally became synonymous with monitoring, compliance, and regulation – almost fulfilling the dystopian dreams of agency theorists. Ironically this association of corporate governance with monitoring neglected the role of boards of directors in supporting strategies for value and growth. Corporate governance is essentially about accountability *and* strategic direction:'The economy depends on the drive and efficiency of its companies. Thus the effectiveness with which their boards discharge their responsibilities determines . . . competitive position. They must be free to drive their companies forward but exercise that freedom within the framework of effective accountability. This is the essence of any system of good governance' (Cadbury 1992: 11).

2.5 One System or Many?

In fact, there are different and contrasting perspectives on corporate governance, which are based on very different understandings of what the purpose of business enterprise actually is. Deriving from these different understandings of business purpose, there are competing corporate governance systems in the market-based Anglo-American system, the European relationship-based system, and the relationship-based system of the Asia Pacific (Clarke 2017; Aguilera & Jackson 2003 and 2010), together with multiple other systems of governance in active development in the emerging economies. An assessment of the wide cross-national diversity of governance institutions and mechanisms was conducted by Schiehll and Martins (2016). The existing and developing rich diversity of corporate governance systems is based on historical, cultural, and institutional dilemmas that involve different approaches to the values and objectives of business activity. When advising on the development of corporate governance principles, the OECD Business Advisory Group (1998: 4) stressed the importance of strategic choice in the determination of governance outcomes:'Entrepreneurs, investors, and corporations need the flexibility to craft governance arrangements that are responsive to unique business contexts so that corporations can respond to necessary changes in technological competition, optimal firm organisation, and vertical networking patterns . . . . To obtain governance diversity, economic regulators, stock exchange rules, and corporate law should support a range of ownership and governance forms.'

This injunction was subsequently largely forgotten by the OECD and other international agencies in their insistence in implying the Anglo-American model as the only reasonable way forward for other countries and regions to adopt. Yet after the signal failures of the Anglo-American governance system in the global financial crisis, and with the advance of the emerging economies, a more pragmatic corporate governance policy emerged from the OECD:

> The regulatory framework must be fit for purpose. And in the complex and multifaceted world of business, this means that regulations must be designed to meet the many varying needs of those entrepreneurs, investors, and stakeholders who are supposed to use them. This is why the G20/OECD *Principles of Corporate Governance* (2015) state that policy makers have a responsibility to establish a regulatory framework that is flexible enough to meet the needs of corporations that operate under widely different circumstances. Only then will it provide market participants with the right incentives to exploit new business opportunities that create value and ensure the most efficient use of capital and other corporate resources. Importantly and in order to support a dynamic business sector, regulations must also be able to accommodate new and innovative business practices. (OECD 2018: 9)

Hence Aquilera et al. (2016) argue there needs to be a degree of freedom for corporate governance practices to be contingent, developing in response to the economic and social context. Potentially there are multiple effective configurations of governance practices with a need to understand the different industry and firm pressures to adopt or differentiate from established practices due to developments in technology, society, finance, and markets. From these processes firms emerge, ranging from the constant creation of a vast mass of small business enterprises, to large complex corporate groups, and to the virtual corporations populating the internet.

Superiority of any one system of governance cannot be accepted as the convergence theorists insist (O'Sullivan (2001); Lane 2004; Clarke 2004a; Clarke 2009). Confidence and trust in the Anglo-American system after successive market crashes cannot be assumed, even if recovery is often quicker than expected (Lorsch 2005). These recurrent crises in the Anglo-American system are interconnected. For example, essentially after the crises of 2001 the US economy was resuscitated by trillions of dollars of cheap debt which in turn caused an unsustainable housing boom, the unwinding of which caused the global financial crisis of 2007-8, with devastating consequences for international financial stability that have persisted to the present day. There is a deep historical tendency in the Anglo-American model to instability and inequity (MacAvoy & Millstein 2004; Clarke 2004b). The advance of structural extreme inequality in the United States and the rest of the world has visibly undermined the stability of the society and economy and badly scarred demo-cratic politics (Picketty 2014; Clarke et al. 2019; Veldman 2019). There is, therefore, a certain inappropriateness in the insistence upon a rapid adoption of this Anglo-American model in all other regimes, as Hansmann and Kraakman (2001) among others once advocated (Mitchell 2001; Clarke & dela Rama 2006; Clarke 2014a).

2.6 The Wide Dimensions of Governance

The competing ideologies and institutional structures that contest the corpor-ate governance space are highlighted by Tricker (2008), one of the pioneers in this field. Historically property rights, managerialist, corporatist, stakeholder, and other conceptions of the understanding of the corporation, its essential structure and mechanisms, and its proper role in the economy and society have wielded influence at different times. Tricker advances a wide perspective:

> The modern enterprise, in reality, is itself loosely bonded and involves complex and interacting networks of relationships. It is better perceived as a set of dynamic open systems – coalitions of interests between parties . . . . Looking ahead the one thing that seems certain is that the existing diversity and complexity of forms of corporate enterprise will continue and, very probably, increase. Alternative paradigms of corporate governance will be needed to improve the effectiveness of governance, to influence the healthy development of corporate regulation, and to understand the reality of the political processes by which companies are governed rather than the structures and mechanisms through which governance is exercised (Tricker 2008: 2,8).

As interest in understanding corporate governance has grown, the question of how this relates to the institutions and practices of public and global governance has arisen: while large corporations are becoming increasingly significant as they operate on a multinational basis, public organizations remain influential in many national sectors, and the role of global institutions has become more critical both for regulation and coordination of the world economy. Apreda (2003) provides a unifying view of governance as a distinctive field of learning and practice, identifying interlinked themes that arise from corporate, public, and global governance, and identifies the core of governance in all three domains as:

i. a founding constitution;
ii. a system of rights and duties;

iii. mechanisms for accountability and transparency;
iv. monitoring and performance measures;
v. stakeholder rights;
vi. good governance standards;
vii. independent gatekeepers.

Returning specifically to corporate governance, Cadbury reminds us of the ethical dimension of corporate values and activity: that firms exist not just for the profit of their immediate owners, but to fulfill a wider social responsibility. The boundaries of what constitutes corporate governance are greatly extended by Turnbull (2012) from the narrow Anglo-American focus on market-oriented publicly traded firms. He claims, 'Corporate governance includes all types of firms whether or not they are formed under civil or common law, owned by the government, institutions, or individuals, privately or publicly traded' (Turnbull 2012: 433). Agency theory is almost entirely concerned with listed companies with unitary boards operating in market systems. However, Turnbull illustrates how the great majority of companies in most economies are not listed on stock exchanges, have compound boards representing diverse shareholder and other stakeholder interests, and have an attenuated relationship to the market. Thus the traditional market-based theory of the firm 'becomes less relevant when economic transactions are mediated by cultural priorities, business related associations, trade, vocational, family, social, and political networks' (Turnbull 2012: 435).

In this context, the finance model of the firm, in which the central problem of corporate governance is how to construct rules and incentives to align the behaviour of managers with the interests of owners, needs to be supplemented with other models of corporate control including the stewardship, stakeholder, and political models applying not simply financial analysis but a cultural and power analysis among other perspectives. For example, from a cultural perspective business dealings, rather than being conducted on the basis of purely rational-legal financial considerations, are 'transactions conducted on the basis of mutual trust and confidence sustained by stable, preferential, particularistic, mutually obligated, and legally non-enforceable relationships. They may be kept together either by value consensus or resource dependency – that is through "culture" and "community" – or through dominant units imposing dependence on others' (Hollingsworth et al. 1994: 6). As Armitage et al. (2017: 150) argue: 'An important implication of such path-dependency, particularly in the context of emerging economies, is that, while regulators and corporate governance activists promote the adoption of international best practices, the differences in formal and informal institutions interact with firm-level governance developments to provide a basis for multidimensional, multi-level corporate governance systems that incorporate the evolution of their country-specific institutions.'

International corporate governance is a set of diverse and contested systems, not a unified and uniform system (Clarke 2005; Clarke & Bostock 1997). The impressive extent to which principles of robust governance and accountability have been diffused around the world and institutionalized in national codes revealed by Enrione et al. (2006), is not matched by confidence that corporate behaviour has changed to the same degree (Clarke 2000; Aguilera & Cuervo-Cazurra 2004).

3 Ownership and Control

3.1 The Separation of Ownership and Control in the United States

The structure of ownership is vital in corporate governance, as it ultimately determines who has the decision-making power in the corporation (Zattoni 2011; Kumar & Zattoni 2015). The fundamental assumption of a universal separation of ownership and control upon which agency theory rests is open to challenge not only in the rest of the world where majority ownership remains deeply embedded, but even in the United States which is portrayed as the archetype of the market-based corporate governance system (La Porta et al. 1999). Zeitlin (2008) offered an early critique of the managerialist theories which proposed the separation of ownership and control, suggesting this meant professional managers had effectively displaced capitalist owners in the running of large corporations. The belief in the disappearance of the control by propri-etary interests of the largest corporations is questioned by the patterns of ownership holdings within and between corporations; the extent of interlocking directorships; the connections with banks and other financial institutions, and who owns these; and the wider networks of ownership and influence.

In fact, large-block shareholders frequently possess the influence and expert-ise to effectively capture property rights and gain control of firms, giving them benefits and rights which are disproportionate to their ownership stakes. In this way a stake of 10 per cent or less in the ownership of shares in a corporation, as the largest shareholder, might be leveraged into effective control of the com-pany. A contingency theory of corporate governance is proposed by Kang and Sorensen (2008), whereby the effect of ownership structure on firm perform-ance is contingent on the fit between owner types and the industry market context, depending on the power relations between organizational participants in relationships that cannot simply be defined in contractual terms.

Defining a controlling shareholder as owning 10 per cent of the voting shares of a corporation directly or through a chain of other shareholdings, Gadhoum et al. (2008) reach the startling conclusion that 59 per cent of listed US corporations have a controlling shareholder, a higher incidence than Japan, and 36 per cent of US corporations are controlled by a family, similar to Germany, and higher than in Japan, France, or the UK. Finally, 24 per cent of US corporations are controlled and managed by a family, similar to East Asia. Therefore, they suggest the principal consequences of strong shareholder protection in the US may be less to prevent professional managers from exploiting dispersed shareholders, than to prevent controlling shareholders from exploiting minority shareholders. The entire focus of agency theory on problems of monitoring management free riding and asymmetric information may help to explain the limited success of successive interventions aimed at managers, when controlling shareholders often represent a greater threat of the expropriation of other interests.

3.2 The Separation of Ownership and Control around the World

The concentration of ownership in the rest of the world is very apparent, and there is significantly less evidence of any separation of ownership and control. Business groups which amalgamate the interests of legally independent companies, through various formal and informal ties, represent the dominant form of large enterprise in emerging markets and remain evident in many parts of Europe (Colli & Colpan 2016; Clarke & Monkhouse 1995). Claessens et al. (2000) extend the analysis of La Porta et al. (1999) in a detailed study of the concentration of ownership and control of 2,980 publicly traded companies in nine East Asian countries.

What is revealed in Claessens et al (2000) is an extensive historical pattern of control enhanced by pyramid structures, cross-holdings among firms, and voting rights exceeding formal ownership share. The concentration of voting rights is critical to the governance of companies since it allows determination of dividend policies, investment projects, executive appointments, and other business strategies. More than two-thirds of firms were controlled by a single shareholder, and the top management of 60 per cent of firms was related to the family of the controlling shareholder. Owners and managers may be different people, but they are not separated. A significant share of national corporate assets was possessed by a small number of families, with 16.6 per cent of all assets in Indonesia, and 17.1 per cent of assets in the Philippines traced to the ultimate control of a single family. In Indonesia, the Philippines, and Thailand ten families had control of half of all corporate assets; and in Hong Kong and

Korea they controlled a third of all corporate assets. This historical concentration of wealth, which continues to a degree to the present day, represents a formidable barrier to the evolution of the legal and institutional reforms of corporate governance and economic activity (Claessens 2004; Claessens et al. 2000).

Though there are many widely held companies in Western Europe, an analysis of ownership structure and the means by which owners gain control rights in excess of their ownership rights by Faccio and Lang (2008) demonstrate that ownership concentration is more extensive. Widely held firms form 36.93 per cent of the listed market in Western Europe, while family-controlled firms are 44.29 per cent of the market. Devices to intensify control are widespread including the use of multiple classes of shares, pyramidal ownership structures, multiple control chains, and cross-holdings. The recent growth of equity markets in Europe, and the related increase in the market for corporate control, might unsettle this pattern of consolidated ownership to a degree in future, but the concentrated pattern of ownership and control is so integral to the economies and societies of Europe it is likely to change slowly. Substantial evidence of a serious movement in the opposite direction exists in the post-Soviet experience in Russia, with the redistribution of vast state-owned industries such as oil and gas into very few private hands. Gurlev and Rachinsky (2008) examine how a small number of oligarchs control a substantial part of the Russian economy. The industrial oligarchs are often considered as the only effective counterweight to a predatory state bureaucracy, though are also seen as stripping the wealth from Russian firms to send overseas, in the process undermining any belief in the viability of a market economy. The oligarchs have contributed to making post-Soviet Russia one of the most inequitable of the developed nations, with the richest ten oligarch families owning 60 per cent of Russia's stock market.

3.3 Family Ownership

Despite the emphasis in the governance literature on the separation of ownership and control for most of the last century, the small family firm remains the predominant form of enterprise universally. 'Family firms as an ownership form dominate both emerging and advanced economies and account for the majority of firms worldwide' (Aguilera et al. 2015: 161; La Porta et al. 1999). The high incidence of family ownership would not be so universal, however, if family-owned firms did not enjoy some distinct and enduring competitive and operational advantages. In fact, family ownership can confer both positive and negative consequences for firm performance (Kumar & Zattoni 2016a).

Historically family-controlled firms have often been associated with nepotism, minority shareholder expropriation, inefficient risk-bearing, and under-investment (Fama & Jensen 1983).

Recently there has been more recognition of family firms' unique cap-acity to accumulate and utilize assets, which accounts for their ubiquity in developing countries where they are often regarded as the engines of the economy (Whyte 1996). Carney (2008) attempts to go beyond this, arguing that organizational value-creating attributes are embedded in the firm's system of corporate governance in which specific incentives, authority structures, and norms of accountability generate particular capabilities. The vast majority of family enterprises remain small and appear best equipped for trading, franchising, and small-scale manufacturing, demon-strating parsimony and efficiency advantages in certain industries. Certainly, family firms demonstrate resilience, in their longevity, stakeholder out-comes, and institutional impacts (van Essen et al. 2015). Assessment of the economic impact of family firms needs to balance their capacity to substitute for numerous institutional voids, especially in developing econ-omies, with their potential to restrain the development of other forms of social and institutional capital.

3.4 Institutional Investors: Reuniting Ownership and Control

In recent times in advanced market economies there has emerged an even greater force for reuniting ownership and control in the rapid and immense growth of the institutional investors. A transformation has occurred in the ownership of corpor-ate equity with individual investors replaced by pension funds, insurance com-panies, and mutual funds. In the US, individuals still held 75 per cent of corporate stock in the early 1970s, but by 2000 institutional owners held 60 per cent of the stock in the largest 1,000 firms. Hawley and Williams (2008) consider how institutional managers have become the fiduciaries of the ultimate beneficiaries, with holdings so diversified that they care not just about the governance and performance of individual companies but about the performance of the economy as a whole. Institutions consider both portfolio-wide issues and economy-wide issues in order to maximize their wealth in the long term and will increasingly look at events and actions not in isolation, but in terms of the effects that may lead to long-term benefits. Inevitably this involves institutions having a regard for wider social, economic, and environmental issues that will impact upon financial returns in the long run, extending their fiduciary duties in the process.

The role of institutions is growing in all the advanced industrial countries as their share of corporate equity increases. Davis (2008) assesses the relation between the growth of institutions, equity finance, corporate governance, and performance. These relationships may be more salient in market-oriented Anglo-American economies, but the influence of the institutional investors is increasing in Europe and Japan. An increasing concentration of assets among a small group of professional investors employed by the institutions has greatly increased the capacity of these large equity holders to exercise influence onboards including over executive compensation, share repurchases, and anti-takeover devices. 'The thrust of the influence has been to increase the vigilance of directors in their role as monitors of management, leading to greater board discipline of management around enhancing total shareholder returns' (Useem 2012).

The growing dominance of equity holdings by institutional investors in Anglo-American countries means the direct influence of the institutions is replacing the previous dependence on the takeover mechanism to discipline managers. Securing improvements in corporate governance may boost the share price and performance of companies the institutions invest in, but also have beneficial consequences at the macro-economic level as managers of all firms alter their behaviour in response to the new business environment. While institutional returns have undoubtedly benefited from this new regime of increased dividend distributions, less fixed investments and higher productivity growth in the corporate sector, questions could be posed whether these strategies are allowing sufficient investment for innovation and future business growth (Lazonick 2007).

However, when analyzing the impact of investor activism, it is important to distinguish the contrasting investment strategies of different types of institutional investor: though often aggregated together the pension funds, insurance companies, and mutual funds have different characteristics and objectives (and, of course, hedge funds and other investment vehicles have markedly different strategies again) (McNulty & Nordberg 2016; Stathopoulos & Voulgaris 2016; Clarke 2007). Ryan and Schneider (2008) distinguish a range of institutional activism from cooperative to hostile and suggest various characteristics that may influence the propensity to activism including the size of the fund, investment time horizon, performance expectations, sensitivity to business relationships, the size of holding, and commitment to active or passive investing.

As a former CEO of a large mutual fund, Bogle (2008) witnessed what he defines as the ascendancy of capitalism that benefits managers at the expense of owners in the late twentieth century and issues a clarion call for greater institutional investor activism. Beyond the legislative and regulatory interventions that were introduced after the Enron debacle, Bogle looks for a change in the orientation of corporate management in the US towards active corporate citizenship, more independent boards, aligning executive stock options with long-term performance, more transparent accountability, and a greater sense of fiduciary duty. This growing sentiment for a reawakened institutional activism represents a real challenge to corporate boards and directors to attend more adequately to their governance responsibilities.

3.5 Institutional Investors and Long-Term Value Creation

The institutional investors are now the major players in all investment asset classes. Pension funds, investment funds, and insurance companies more than doubled their total assets under management from USD 36 trillion in 2000 to USD 73.4 trillion in 2011 and have continued growing rapidly since, with PWC (2020) estimating assets under management at in excess of USD 100 trillion. Investment in global stock markets remains the largest asset class invested in for pension funds and investment funds, however the increase in the assets of the investors has outstripped the growth of global stock markets (Çelik & Isaksson 2014: 97).

The growing economic significance and market power of institutional investors suggests they may be central to the future transformation of corporate governance. The institutional investors' simultaneous and contradictory desires for the immediate results of short-term returns, sustained performance, and corporate social responsibility are creating corporate governance confusion. As the power of the institutions expands further, either they could become an irresistible force for further economic instability induced by short-termism, or they could impress upon markets' and companies' longer-term horizons, and the pursuit of sustainability. The implications of the increasing scale and activity of the institutional investors upon corporate governance have yet to be fully understood and appreciated including:

- the complex relationships that exist across the institutional investment sector, in which corporate governance will play a greater role as the funds under the control of these institutions further increase;
- the increasing sophistication of the corporate governance policies of the institutional investors;
- the significance of the institutions' own governance as they seek to influence the entities in which they invest, and the criticality of the governance of the investment value chain, the complexities of which have often remained hidden;
- the efficiency and effectiveness of existing methods of institutional investor participation in corporate governance, including voting procedures, the

conduct of annual general meetings (AGMs), and other forms of corporate engagement with institutional shareholders;

- the nature of investment institutions' trustees' roles, resources, and expertise in carrying out their responsibilities; and
- how in carrying out their fiduciary duties institutional investor principals and agents exercise their discretion with regard to investment risk, performance, investment horizons, and sustainability (Clarke 2017: 152).

As John Rogers of the CFA Institute insists, 'The future of finance needs to be less about leverage, financial engineering, and stratospheric bonuses and more about efficiently and cleanly connecting capital with ideas, long-term investing for the good of society, and delivering on promises to future generations' (RIAA 2015: 1).

In this context, two kinds of investor activism at opposite ends of the spectrum need to be carefully distinguished, ranging from the speed of the electronic reflexes of the high-frequency traders (Clarke 2014c), to the long-term commitments of values-based investors:

- short-term, often secretive, but sometimes highly publicized, shareholder activism focused upon immediate returns for themselves; and
- the wider shareholder activism movement pressing for long-term value creation, responsible corporations, and the best interests of all stakeholders including shareholders.

This wider and more values-based responsible movement is continuing to grow in scale and significance, even if it does not secure frequent headlines in the financial press (Clarke 2017: 179).

4 Boards and Directors

The board of directors is the epicentre of corporate governance, the arena in which all of the mechanisms of governance are required to respond to market signals, institutional pressures, and strategic possibilities in order to secure the commercial viability and accountability of the business (Huse 2007 and 2018). The evident fact that boards of directors often do not live up to these great expectations is one of the continuing dilemmas of corporate governance. Whenever a major corporation fails, the first resounding question is, 'Where was the board?' The disappointing answer is that if the board of directors were not asleep at the wheel, they certainly did not demonstrate the strategic alertness or fiduciary commitment that ostensibly they were there to provide (Clarke 2017).

The contribution of boards of directors is widely recognized, and invariably boards are established to govern large and complex corporations in both the private and public sector. But also boards of directors are universally adopted in smaller organizations in public service, and in the professional, commercial, and voluntary sectors. Yet the evidence concerning boards' contribution to corporate governance and performance is not clear: 'Evidence concerning direct relationships between board attributes and corporate performance is scant, ambiguous, and not conclusive' (Adams et al. 2010: 58). The interdependencies between boards and firm performance are complex and require a number of theoretical perspectives to comprehend in an integrated way (Daily et al. 2003).

However, integrating different theoretical approaches is only possible when the underlying assumptions fit. Major approaches to the analysis of board effectiveness include a structural approach of finance and economics informed by agency theory that focuses on attributes such as board size and composition; and management and organizational research focusing either on board relationships or board behaviour informed from a sociological or social-psychological perspective. Fundamental differences in the perspectives include assumptions about rational and self-interested behaviour; the emphasis or neglect of fundamental contingencies in corporate governance and the heterogeneity of corporations; the significance of the interdependencies of corporate governance institutions at national level that impact on board characteristics; how board direction and characteristics are endogenous and the result of strategic choice; and how board research has tended to take boards as monolithic entities when they are composed of individuals operating in a team, with implications for the performance of individuals and boards (van Ees & van der Laan 2012).

All boards necessarily are based on creative tension, exhibiting the capacity to question and challenge, as well as to support and sustain. Frequently the greatest source of tension is between what the board of directors believes is its legitimate desire to exercise ultimate control of the company, and management's determination to retain what it defines as the necessary level of operational control of the business (Demb & Neubauer 1992; Carter & Lorsch 2004). Usually this tension is interpreted through an agency perspective of the need to discipline managers to deliver value to shareholders involving:

> The agency conflicts among the different agents related to the firm and the effectiveness of the internal and external control mechanisms in inducing managerial value enhancing actions. These controls traditionally have been classified as internal or external. Internal controls principally include the board of directors and mutual monitoring among managers (Fama 1980; Fama & Jensen 1983), the direct managerial share ownership (Jensen & Meckling 1976), the use of variable managers' remuneration schemes, the supervisory role played by the large shareholders (Demsetz and Lehn 1985), and the use of debt financing (Jensen 1986). External controls are exerted by

the market for corporate control (Grossman & Hart 1980), the managerial labour market (Fama, 1980), and the product market (Hart, 1983). (Fernandez & Arrondo 2005: 857)

4.1 Directors' Duties and Agency Theory

The doctrine that corporations must be managed to maximize shareholders' returns took firm hold by the early 1990s and helped induce large corporations to pursue increasingly risky financial strategies in their relentless drive to enhance shareholder value. Yet contrary to popular myth, corporate law in no jurisdiction internationally requires corporate directors to maximize shareholder value. It is mythological that corporate law in the United States incorporates shareholder primacy or shareholder value (Blair 2012; Stout 2012). Corporate law in the US and UK states that they must act 'in the best interests of the corporation' (Bratton and Wachter 2010). The shareholder primacy doctrine claims that shareholder value maximization is the singular social and economic goal of the corporation because it maximizes the overall wealth being created by the corporation, disciplining management to this metric.

However, shareholder value can be increased not by adding to the social wealth generated by the enterprise for all stakeholders, but by extracting value from other stakeholders. 'The idea that maximising shareholder value is equivalent to maximising the total social value created by a firm seems obviously wrong to anyone who observes the various ways that corporations can (and do) externalise some of their costs onto employees, customers, or the communities in which they operate' (Blair 2012: 64). The flawed principles of shareholder value have structurally undermined the institutions and practices of corporate governance and contributed to a long series of corporate governance disasters, including the global financial crisis.

The pursuit of shareholder value has critically weakened the capacity of the corporation to generate value for the longer term, and often persuades directors to sanction high-risk strategies for short-term returns. Commitment to the shareholder value doctrine can prove irresponsible and dangerous (Aglietta & Reberious 2005; Gelter 2009). Bratton and Wachter (2010) argue that firms that were most influenced by market pressures to increase their share price in the years leading up to the financial crisis were the firms that recklessly increased their leverage and were most impacted by the global financial crisis.

Directors do have the authority and responsibility in law to consider the interests of all stakeholders in the corporate enterprise, and to find outcomes of value to all parties (Blair 2012). Blair and Stout (1999) have outlined an alternative team production theory of corporate governance and directors' duties which recognizes that productive activity requires multiple parties to contribute to the enterprise in complex and integrated ways. This perspective allows directors to recognize and value the contributions of all who engage in pursuing the success of the business enterprise. The board is identified here as a critical coordinating body, tasked to represent and mediate between all stakeholders that add value, assume unique risk, and possess strategic information critical for firm operations (Kaufmann & Englander 2005).

This extended team production approach rests upon a conception of the firm as a nexus of team-specific assets invested by stakeholders. These investments create valuable resources that are difficult for other companies to emulate, and create competitive advantage and higher returns for firms in possession of these unique resources (Barney 1991; Wang & Barney 2006). The board itself attributes important capabilities to the process of value creation in the firm, including relational, firm, and market analytical and functional abilities. These dynamic capabilities of boards represent the ability to reconfigure internal and external assets and competencies, in order to address the challenges of changing external environments (Teece & Pitelis 2009).

4.2 Who Controls the Company?

There is almost universally a degree of tension between the board and management, which can be productive or negative. The outcome of this tension is generally believed to be that though the board does have formal power over management, in practice management dominates the board. Mizruchi (2003) offers a different view, insisting the board of directors remains the ultimate centre of control. The degree of control may vary depending on the relative performance of the firm, as boards tend to become more involved at times of crisis. Board members may not be involved with the day to day management or have a close interest in the more technical aspects of the company, however they possess 'bottom line control' in setting a framework within which management must operate, and in retaining the power to hire and fire the chief executive if management does not perform accordingly. (Indeed, in recent decades the average tenure of CEOs of US corporations has fallen dramatically in a context of greater competitiveness and uncertainty to which boards may have contributed.) Weir et al. (2008) identify the external as well as internal governance mechanisms that may discipline management, highlighting the continuing impact of the market for corporate control as a disciplinary mechanism, and insisting the relationship between governance mechanisms and company performance is a complex one, calling for more flexibility in the development of company-specific governance structures appropriate for companies at different stages in their life-cycle, and operating in different markets.

The growing number of shareholder proposals to company annual meetings represents a further resilient disciplining force upon both boards and management. Loring and Taylor (2006) illustrate how institutional investors have enjoyed increasing success in impressing their views through the proxy process on issues such as executive compensation and poison pills. Finally, Fernandez and Arrondo (2005) emphasize the existence of multiple alternatives of control, arguing the composition and impact of the board is influenced by the intensity of the control provided by other mechanisms including the incentive effects of managerial stock ownership, and the supervision exercised by large shareholders.

A further dimension of board/management relations is revealed by Baysinger and Hoskisson (1990), who investigate how board composition and governance orientation may influence the strategic decision-making process and strategic outcomes in large corporations. Strategic effectiveness involves achieving an alignment between control strategies and the strategic context of the firm. Business strategies involving substantial risk require internal controls that are rich in information and involve open and subjective corporate relations. In contrast, lower-risk strategies can be managed using more formal and objective controls. For example, Hoskisson and Hitt (1988) found reliance on formal financial controls and incentives is negatively associated with the extent of research and development intensity. While outsider-dominated boards may be appropriate in larger, diversified corporations, it is possible more insider-based boards are appropriate for small R & D-intensive firms.

Stiles and Taylor (2002) examine further the board's role in strategic decision-making. The board's role is not to formulate strategy, but to set the context for strategic thinking, and to review management's strategic proposals, changing these if necessary. This central role attributed to the board in the strategic process is contrary to the managerialist view of the passivity of the board:

> Firstly, the board is the ultimate arbiter of what constitutes the focus of the company ('what business are we in?', 'what areas should we go into?'). Secondly, through selective screening and confidence building, the capacity for innovation and entrepreneurship can be regulated. Thirdly, through constant examination of the business definition and corporate strategy, the commitment to certain strategies or business sectors may be questioned and so boards may be instrumental in breaking organizational habits and forcing change (Stiles & Taylor 2002: 52).

The roles of boards of directors in strategic direction have changed over time, and in different contexts. For example, historically boards have needed to take firm control of company strategy at times of crisis, even if they did not do so before. Research on boards from the 1970s onwards focused on the relative passivity of boards, and how they were frequently subject to managerial hegemony (Mace 1971). By the early 1990s, agency theory became the dominant framework for the analysis of the contribution of boards, utilizing quantitative data, but indicating uncertainty regarding consequences of board involvement (Fama & Jensen 1983; Sundaramerthy & Lewis 2003). From the 2000s onwards, though agency theory remained influential, analysis from a behavioural perspective including stakeholder, resource dependency, and stewardship theory became common. These approaches focus on boards' participation and contribution to strategic decision-making and outcomes utilizing qualitative research to understand more about the inner dynamics of boards and their relationship with management (Pugliese & Zattoni 2012; Huse 2007; Hillman et al. 2009). Boards of directors are now subject to greater scrutiny regarding their influence and decisions, and evidence regarding board and company performance more critically examined.

4.3 Maintaining Balance: The Role of the Chair

If the board is to exercise a strategic role and to provide accountability, the position of chair of the board assumes greater significance. In the US this role was often combined with the CEO's job, constituting a duality in which the CEO not only runs the company, but also guides the board through its governance responsibilities. In the UK, Europe, and most other jurisdictions (and increasingly in the US) the roles have been separated in large public corporations as together they represent a considerable concentration of power. This division of responsibilities permits a balance of power and authority, ensuring no individual has unfettered decision-making power. Cadbury, in his leadership of the UK Committee on the Financial Aspects of Corporate Governance (1992), was instrumental in encouraging this separation of powers internationally, as other countries adopted similar codes of corporate governance.

The division of powers is normally that the chair is responsible for the board, and all of its duties, and the chief executive is responsible for the running of the company. However, this clear delineation of roles may often be less clear in practice, and depends on the relationship of the two individuals, and their relationship with the rest of the board. Coles and Hesterly (2000) explore further the effects of different governance arrangements at board level, examining leadership structure and the influence of outside directors. They propose that the independence of the chair is a determinant of how the market views the actions of the company (in this instance, the acceptability of the adoption of poison pill defences), and if the chair is not independent, then the monitoring and control function of outside directors becomes more critical.

4.4 The Struggle for Independence: Non-executive Directors

Independent directors are increasingly seen as central to the reform of corporate governance, and codes of practice increasingly suggest there should be a majority of independent directors on the boards of listed companies. The emphasis on the independence of directors as the apparent priority over other considerations is often criticized by business leaders. Matolcsy et al. (2004) indicate that companies investing in growth involving research and development and intangibles not always recognized on the balance sheet do benefit from having a greater proportion of independent directors on their boards. Actual board effectiveness depends on the behavioural dynamics of the board (Veltrop et al. 2017). Roberts et al. (2005) suggest it is critical how the interpersonal relationships between executive and non-executive directors develop in a company context. Non-executives both support executives and monitor their conduct, challenging and questioning, and drawing on their experience in support of executive performance. In this way non-executives maintain their confidence in the performance of the company, the development of strategy, and the adequacy of reporting and risk assessment.

The *Harvard Law Review* proposes a resolution of the incipient development of a structural divide between 'independent' and 'non-independent' directors, that rather than independence being the lonely province of outside directors, independence as a norm should encompass all directors. A functional conception of director independence that balances the normative goals of independence-based reforms with the behavioural constraints faced by modern boards is suggested. The existing models of independence including the disinterested outsider, objective monitor, and unaffiliated professional require rethinking to extend to the collective efforts of every director the commitment to clear accountability and informational transparency.

However, the degree of independence of directors may be questioned if they are representative of one small section of the community (once referred to as pale, male, and stale). The lack of diversity on boards of directors is now an issue internationally. The gender imbalance on boards is presently being met both by voluntary targets for increasing the participation of women on boards, and by mandatory quotas that offer more immediate solutions (Klettner et al. 2016). However, the gender imbalance of boards of directors is only one element of a lack of diversity of skills, experience, ethnicity, and age on one-dimensional boards (OECD 2019).

4.4 Devolving Power: Nomination and Succession Committees

Large listed companies have developed nomination and succession committees to identify new directors. Yet the most important succession in any company, and often the least planned, is that of the chief executive. Despite decades of governance reform, the preparedness with which companies embark on a wide search and selection of their new CEO is often minimal (the tradition was a tap on the shoulder of a designated candidate after brief discussion between those in the inner circle). Datta et al. (2002) examine the organizational factors that influence the desirability of the type of experience that a new CEO will bring to the job, and highlight firm profitability, size, and advertising intensity as key. Directors will affirm the status quo when financial indices are good.C onversely when profitability is falling, internal candidates will be perceived as part of the problem rather than likely to offer a solution, whereas outsiders will be regarded as offering a fresh perspective. Size is associated with organizational complexity, which heightens the need for organizational familiarity, and may mean a larger pool of talent from which to identify a successor. With regard to replenishing the board, Ruigrok et al. (2006) examine how nomination committees are now entrusted with identifying and proposing new board members that will raise boards' capability and independence, though to a lesser degree board diversity.

4.5 Evaluating Executives: The Remuneration Committee

The most serious dilemma in contemporary corporate governance is undoubtedly the explosion in the remuneration of CEOs of large US corporations over the last two decades. This rampant inflation in CEO reward is apparently unrelated to performance, and has influenced levels of CEO reward internationally. Remuneration committees of the board of directors were intended to deal with this problem. Conyon and Peck (1998) review the impact of having remuneration committees composed entirely of non-executive directors on executive reward in the UK and conclude that there is little evidence of this resulting in a downward revision of the level of management pay. However, an independent remuneration committee is associated with achieving a closer alignment of management pay and corporate performance.

Investors often view executive compensation arrangements as a window on the overall quality of the governance of corporations and attach great importance to the independence of the members of compensation committees of public companies. Wood (2004) elaborates the evolution of independence requirements of different regulators in the US including the SEC, NYSE, and NASDAQ, raising the bar of what constitutes independence, and removing the protection of the business judgment rule protection for directors who fail to confirm that the actions they approve are in the best interests of the company. The former chairman of the International Corporate Governance Network of institutional investors, Alistair Ross Goobey (2005), was sceptical about the restraining influence of the reform of executive compensation in the face of the scale of the problem, and the potential impact of the US levels of reward: 'The difference between US and UK levels of remuneration became especially pronounced in 1997, a year in which the top executives of the largest 500 UK companies earned a total of $500 million, and Disney's Michael Eisner exercised options worth $576 million and was awarded another 24 million options with an estimated "worth" at issue of more than $200 million'(Goobey 2005: 37). Goobey concluded soberly the best that can be hoped for is that greater transparency, better analysis, and more shareholders monitoring may make it less possible for poorly structured remuneration packages to be approved.

Better metrics are essential if executive reward is to be gauged more rigorously, to provide better information to measure and manage corporate and executive performance. Yet accounting-based measures such as earnings and return on investment measure only one aspect of performance, and it is possible to manipulate more easily single performance indicators than a broader set of metrics offering a greater strategic assessment of the direction a company is traveling. Epstein and Roy (2005) offer a more balanced business scorecard developing governance sophistication in the evaluation of the performance of boards and CEOs around critical dimensions of long-term corporate performance including finance, strategy, customer relations, risk management, operations, human resources, ethics, and innovation.

4.6 Internal Control: The Audit Committee

Audit committees are considered another bastion of governance establishing a link between the external auditor and the board, reducing the risk of illegal activity and preventing fraudulent financial reporting. But the effectiveness of corporate auditing is open to question (Clarke an&& d Dean 2007). Spira (1999) suggests there is little evidence that audit committees will protect auditor independence and lead to improved financial reporting; rather they tend to serve a ceremonial function providing an external symbol of legitimacy. Turley and Zaman (2004) also question the evidence of a link between audit committees and financial reporting quality, commenting that though there are a number of potential impacts on aspects of internal control, internal audit, and risk management, there is little understanding of how these impacts are achieved. More needs to be known about the complex environment in which audit committees operate, and their interaction with other parties including executive management and external auditors. For example, Vera-Munoz (2005) examines the effectiveness of audit committees in a highly charged corporate governance environment where there are high expectations of their capacity to protect investors' interests.

5 Executives and Performance

Attention has been focused upon the importance of the role of corporate executives since Berle and Means first elaborated their thesis of the separation of ownership and control early in the twemtieth century. Successive commentators acknowledged the key importance of the new technocratic management in control of the modern corporation (Galbraith 1968) and chronicled the ascendancy of managerial capitalism in American business (Chandler 1977). The public prominence of business executives developed as the twentieth century progressed, but it was only in the final decades of the century that the CEO, particularly in the largest US corporations, became such an imperial figure (it is a little ironic that this elevation of CEOs occurred during the era of supposed shareholder primacy). CEOs have become increasingly responsible for defining and projecting the objectives of corporations, and as a consequence have claimed an increasing share of rewards and recognition (Boyer 2005; Clarke 2014b). In turn, most dramatically at times of corporate failure, CEO power, performance, and compensation have become subject to intense public scrutiny.

5.1 Agency Dilemmas

The new-found prominence of corporate executives from the 1970s coincided with the advance of agency theory. Fama (1980) extends the view of the firm as a set of contracts among factors of production elaborated by Alchian and Demsetz (1972) and Jensen and Meckling (1976), recognizing the separation of ownership and control, and treating risk bearing and management as separate factors within the set of firm contracts. The firm is disciplined by competition from other firms, which forces the evolution of devices for monitoring the performance of management. A succession of devices have been recommended by agency theorists for the effective monitoring of management, most notably the discipline of the capital market with leveraged takeovers (which led executives to make further efforts to entrench themselves), and the introduction of stock options to align executive interests with shareholders (which led to a massive inflation of executive reward unrelated to performance), both of which largely achieved the opposite of their intended effect.

A more recent hope has been that institutional investors might effectively monitor the performance of the CEOs of the largest corporations in which they have become the majority shareholders. Coffee (1991) pours cold water on this aspiration: 'The famous generalization of Berle and Means that the modern public corporation produced the separation of ownership and control can be translated into the deeper and more accurate statement that the public shareholders in the modern corporation purchased liquidity at the cost of control' (Coffee 1991: 1330). He sees unstable and shifting coalitions among the institutional investors themselves and between majority shareholders and the management. However, Coffee recognizes some institutional investors may prove more effective in the monitoring role: institutions with large equity stakes prepared to hold over the longer term and without substantial conflicts of interest.

The Enron implosion and associated large corporate collapses in the US in 2001-2, if ostensibly evidence of the worst fears of agency theorists, was emblematic of the failure of agency theory to find any solution to market and incentive systems that encouraged the rampant self-interest of executives. Arnold and de Lange (2004) illustrate how Enron's executives circumvented the mechanisms supposed to discipline them, and how the market ignored the risks Enron was taking, analysts and investors preferring to believe the rampant optimism of Enron's CEO pronouncements. Replacing the arrogant and self-interested management culture of Enron, some have called for a different approach to corporate governance.

The traditional forms of corporate governance based on assumptions of hierarchy and bureaucracy have to come to terms with new forms of business enterprise in which there are multiple agency dilemmas, in more flexible businesses based on networks and alliances. In these new forms of enterprise a democratization of rights and voice is required, with more inclusive and transparent systems of control, and mutual monitoring to promote trust. It should not be left to the bravery of a few individual whistle-blowers, as in the case of Enron and WorldCom, to reveal corporate malfeasance; effective systems are necessary to give earlier warning than this.

5.2 Firm Performance

In the context of corporate failure the focus of corporate governance is upon accountability, however another critical dimension is how corporate governance might contribute to firm performance. The relationship between corporate governance and performance is complex, and researchers have struggled with multiple variables, and often been disappointed in searching for a 'governance effect' in share price behaviour following changes in the composition of company boards or CEOs, or takeover defences (Gugler 2001; Clarke 2007: 119). The balance of recent longitudinal studies in the US demonstrates that high governance risk correlates with lower performance, and robust governance is associated with more sustained performance (Gompers et al. 2003). In Europe and Asia, companies with higher standards of governance were discovered to have higher performance in large samples of companies (Drobetz et al. 2004; Bauer & Guenster 2003). One of the more difficult things in assessing the influence of corporate governance upon firm performance is to take into account the impact of changes in the market: at times of rapid market expansion many companies will perform well, in times of market recession most companies will find it more difficult to perform. In economic theory at least, boards and executives are rewarded on how well they interpret and respond to market changes, however in practice – particularly at times of great volatility – it is often more likely that the momentum of the market simply carries executives and their companies along.

Examining the governance of state enterprises, Bozec (2005) finds that market competition is positively related to firm profitability and productivity, and that it is in competitive environments that boards most effectively contribute to performance. Certo et al. (2006) investigate the contribution of top management teams to firm performance, addressing the debate between those who maintain that the influence of the composition of the top management is fundamental to firm performance, and those who insist that the market environment shapes firm performance and that the influence of executives is tenuous. Certo et al. (2006) find that top management teams can provide more information processing capacity and greater functional heterogeneity, which contribute to firm performance. However, strategic variables that impact on the relationship between executives and performance included diversification, research and development expenditure, and internationalization: a top executive team composition was required to be able to cope with the complexity of these strategic choices.

5.3 Executive Compensation I: Central Concerns

Accepting the complex demands of the executive role in large corporations does not necessarily justify the extraordinarily large reward packages that American CEOs now claim. As Elhagrasey et al. (1998: 312) insist: 'It is difficult to imagine how the highly publicized eight-digit compensation figures for some top corporate executives can serve shareholder interests or could be derived from rational compensation schemes. Some form of CEO influence seems obvious, and seems to be overcoming efforts by the SEC, state governments, institutional investors, and other interest groups to regulate compensation.'

Elhagrasey et al. (1998) explain unrestrained CEO pay as a result of CEO power over boards of directors, including CEO use of co-optation, outside experts, remuneration committees, and the selective use of criteria to control the compensation process and rationalize and legitimize their compensation.

Matsumura and Shin (2005) examine the intended and unintended consequences of widely proposed executive compensation reforms including greater independence for compensation committees; requiring executives to hold equity in the corporation; greater disclosure of executive compensation; increased institutional investor involvement; and requiring firms to expense stock options. They conclude that whatever remedies these proposals might offer given the intrinsic limitations of regulatory actions intended to discipline executive pay, what is required is a stronger ethical framework which redefines corporate objectives and takes account of the interests of a broader group of stakeholders. Conyon (2006) analyzes the development of executive pay in the United States, in the context of the debate between the agency model which suggests shareholders (through the compensation committee of the board) design executive pay contracts using stock options; restricted stock and long-term incentives to motivate CEOs to maximize firm value; and the managerial power view which proposes that the CEO and board agree compensation contracts not in shareholders interests, but to maximize CEO reward. Conyon (2006: 27) highlights the correlation between CEO pay and firm size, stressing that '[t]he notion that all CEOs receive stratospheric sums is incorrect'. The distribution of CEO compensation is that a relatively few CEOs of larger companies earn vast sums, with the great majority of CEOs in small enterprises earning more modest amounts.

While there are a number of explanations for the growth of executive compensation (Kumar & Zattoni 2016) – including greater risk and incentives; shifts in the managerial labor market; changes in board compensation practices; shifts in corporate strategy, technology, and the business environment; misconceptions about the cost and value of options; as well as managerial control of the compensation process – it is hard to escape the conclusion that executive compensation is a central part of the problem rather than a solution to corporate governance dilemmas. Instead of a land of opportunity, America is becoming typified as a land of extreme inequality, with the CEO to worker compensation ratio exploding, from 20 to 1 in the 1960s to 100 to 1 in the 1990s, peaking at 344 to 1 in the tech bubble of 2000, and after a short rise and fall before and after the financial crisis returning to 312 to 1 in 2017. While this phenomenal growth in CEO reward continued, basic wages stagnated in the US for decades and employment security declined (Figure 2).

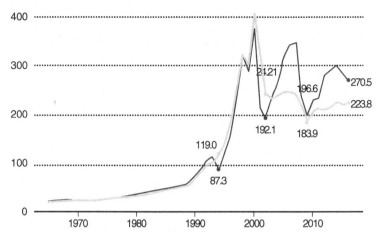

Figure 2 Executive pay as a multiple of worker pay in the US, 1965–2016

Light Blue – executive stock options granted; Dark Blue – executive stock
options realized.

CEO compensation in the top 350 US companies by annual sales. Worker
compensation is the annual average of the workers in the key industry of the
firms in the sample.

Sources: Adapted from Economic Policy Institute (2018); Compustat ExecComp database; and US Bureau of Labour

5.4 Executive Compensation II: Further Controversies

From the 1980s onwards, the largest part of executive remuneration in the US
has been in stock options, meaning the level of executive reward is essentially
determined by stock prices. Frey and Osterloh (2005) explore the unfortunate
implications of this in managements' inclinations to manipulate short-term
profitability to spike share prices and seize exorbitant rewards. In attacking
the extreme inequity that has crept into the American corporation in the
increasingly huge disparity of rewards between CEOs and average wages,
they conceptualize the corporation as a common pool of firm-specific resources
rather than a nexus of individual contracts, characterized by a high degree of
complex interdependencies, citing Simon (1991: 33): 'In general, the greater the
interdependence among various members of the organization, the more difficult
it is to measure their separate contributions to the achievement of organizational
goals. But of course, intense interdependence is precisely what makes it advantageous to organize people instead of depending wholly on market transactions.' Frey and Osterloh (2005) argue that high-powered executive incentive
systems aggravate the problems in the corporate sector, encouraging dysfunctional behaviour and ultimately damaging the firm.

Bebchuk and Fried (2005) agree that managerial influence over compensation schemes has weakened managers' incentives to increase firm value, and created incentives to engage in actions that reduce long-term value. They argue that flawed compensation schemes are widespread, persistent, and systemic in the US and stem from defects in the underlying governance structures; they call for structural reforms in the allocation of power between boards and shareholders. Continuing with this theme, Bebchuk and Jackson (2005) focus on opaqueness in the construction of executive pension schemes which lead to distortions of the magnitude and make-up of total pay, calling for greater disclosure on an annual basis of the monetary value of executive pension entitlements. Pension plans can represent a substantial part of executive total compensation, and the concealment of large elements of these may undermine any effort to link reward to performance.

5.5 CEO Power

In political models of the firm, the interests and beliefs of a dominant coalition preside with CEOs exercising formal authority and informal power. Ocasio (1994) examines the political dynamics of the executive control over the firm's coalition reflected in the ability of CEOs to retain their positions, putting forward the thesis that contesting coalitions are more likely to emerge during periods of poor performance. This model of power builds upon theories of the circulation of elites developed by Pareto (1991) and Michels (2001), introduced to organizational analysis by Selznick (1957). The concept of a circulation of power indicates the impermanence and contestation of executive control over the corporation, contrasting with the theory of institutionalization, which emphasizes the power of CEOs to entrench themselves, providing two views of the capacity of CEOs to maintain cohesive coalitions providing a stable basis for the exercise of power.

In different cultures the evident power of the CEO may not be so great, for example in Japan the CEO apparently is not as prominent as in Western companies. However, this is not to suggest Japanese CEOs have little power, only that there are differences in how Japanese CEOs acquire and exercise power (Seki & Clarke 2014). Slow promotion and job rotation provides Japanese managers with the opportunity to acquire expert influence and build extensive networks and wield influence that can be enduring.

Bird (1990) recounts how successive promotions legitimate the exercise of power, and CEO power is moderated by factors that influence the extent of legitimacy accorded both the individual and the office. Bigley and Wiersma (2002) assess the factors influencing whether newly appointed CEOs' strategic orientation leads them to use their power to maintain the status quo or refocus the firm business portfolios. The relative advantages of an internally appointed CEO compared to an outside CEO are considered by Georgakakis and Ruigrok (2017). Finally, Adams et al. (2005) discover that firm performance becomes more variable as decision-making power becomes more concentrated in the hands of the CEO, compared to firms in which decisions are a product of executive consensus.

6 Stakeholders

A powerful countervailing influence to imperial CEOs is the increasing activity of other stakeholders and the new imperatives of responsibility and sustainability. A renewed force for stakeholder engagement has developed, led by the institutional investors. The dilemma yet to be resolved is whether the institutional investors will translate their success in pressing for better returns for their investments (Davis 2001), into a wider campaign for greater corporate social and environmental responsibility (Davis 2006). The UNEP Financial Initiative is indicative of a new commitment to socially responsible investing, which is resonating in the corporate sector (World Business Council for Sustainable Development 2014, 2015, and 2020; World Economic Forum 2014, 2018, and 2020; Sullivan and Mackenzie 2006)). This is creating a business context in which corporations are demonstrating greater commitment in the exercise and measurement of corporate social responsibility. A more active stakeholder involvement has the potential to contribute to redefining corporate values, activities, and objectives (Post 2002; Clarke 2017).

6.1 The Engagement of Institutional Investors

A new era of institutional investor engagement was recognized by Clark and Hebb (2004) bringing together underlying currents in global pension fund investing, that has continued till the present day (Edwards et al. 2018). This includes the stimulus from investing in the whole market index, meaning that funds cannot exit, and therefore must find a voice in the firms they invest in; the collaboration with the wider corporate governance movement to secure greater corporate transparency and accountability; the growing impact of the socially responsible investment movement; and the internationalization of social, environmental, and accounting standards. The corporate engagement by institutions potentially can help anchor capital to communities, civilize human resource practices within firms, and encourage compliance with labour and environmental standards. If institutional investors are to play an increasingly influential role in corporate governance, it is inevitable and proper that the institutions' own governance should come under more critical scrutiny. Useem and Mitchell (2000) examine the relationship between the governance structures of pension funds and their investment strategies and investment performance. They find that the way public pension funds are governed has a direct bearing on how they invest their assets, and the investment strategies in turn directly shape financial performance. In the United States, pension funds are the fastest growing institutional investors and by 1999 held 42 per cent of US corporate equity controlled by institutions, which has continued to increase further (Çelik & Isaksson 2014). Ryan and Dennis (2003) examine further the complex ethical undertakings and implications of pension funds activities.

In contrast, Clearfield (2005) concentrates attention on the failure of institutional investors to achieve their real potential to exercise governance oversight due to structural factors in the governance of the complex investment value chain, for example, the long-term horizon involved in many corporate governance initiatives; the different backgrounds, aptitudes, and incentives of corporate governance specialists, investment managers, and company executives; reliance on third-party agents; and different career paths and competition for performance compensation. Greater alignment of governance and investment policies, incentives, and commitments would lead to better corporate governance outcomes and portfolio returns.

Perhaps the renewed pension fund insistence upon increased transparency not only will align managers and owners more effectively, but will allow other stakeholders to engage the corporation over their concerns, claiming that when organizations are opaque and interests are secret, decision-making distorts efficiency and equity.

6.2 The Activism of Institutional Investors

As the influence of institutional investors extends internationally, the direction of the impact of their activism becomes more critical. Neubaum and Zahra (2006) pursue in greater detail the debate on whether institutional investors are narrowly interested only in maximizing their short-term financial performance or are capable of a long-term perspective and promoting corporate social performance as well as financial performance. Data collected between 1995 and 2000 for Fortune 500 firms show that long-term institutional ownership is positively associated with enhanced corporate social performance, and the interaction with long-term institutional shareholders has a positive effect on future corporate social performance. The agenda of shareholder activism was partly shaped in the United States on issues such as international human rights and labour standards, suggest that religious groups helped to establish the legitimacy of the agenda, and mobilized support of investors. From this debate it may be concluded that while Anglo-American institutional investors may be influential in Asian and European companies in eroding traditional stake-holder relationships in favour of enhancing shareholder value, institutional investors with longer-term holdings such as pension funds may have a positive effect on influencing more responsible management within Anglo-American markets, and to a degree in the activity of Anglo-American corporations overseas.

The changing pattern of corporate governance activism and influence in Japan is examined by Seki (2005 and 2019). Traditionally Japanese corporate governance was characterized by cross-shareholdings between banks and client companies organized into conglomerates. The executive boards of the compan-ies, composed of present and former managers, were oriented towards the interests of employees, customers, and regulators rather than shareholders. While central elements of this pattern of insider governance remain, the chan-ging ownership structure with a larger institutional investor representation, particularly from overseas institutions, has put new pressures on Japanese boards to deliver shareholder value. The implications of this for the good relationships Japanese companies have enjoyed with other stakeholders and for the value system sustaining this are presently contested (Buchanan et al. 2014; Seki & Clarke 2015; Yoshikawa 2018).

6.3 Governance and Employees

The interests of employees are conventionally excluded from discussion of contemporary corporate governance in Anglo-American economies, except as an afterthought when the suggestion is often made that the pursuit of share-holder value will inevitably serve the interests of other stakeholders as value creation requires the engagement of all stakeholders (Blair & Roe 1999; Clarke 1998). The problematic nature of this assumption is experienced in high relief in countries such as Japan, where employees' interests have traditionally been foremost in company orientations (Learmont 2002; Jacoby 2004). Takeshi (2001) investigates the implications of the corporate governance reforms in Japan in terms of the movement from a pluralist model of corporate governance, where the objective of the firm is to realize all stakeholder interests, to an enlightened shareholder value model to pursue shareholder value by engaging stakeholders in accomplishing this objective. Though Japanese employers insist they remain committed to a pluralist approach, there is evidence they are increasingly pursuing enlightened share-holder value in eroding the employment seniority system, widening wage differentials, diversifying wage systems, and undermining working conditions (Seki & Clarke 2014).

Blair (1999) takes issue with the property rights view of the firm as a bundle of assets belonging to shareholders and managed by their hired agents. An alternative view of the firm is that the relationships among the people who participate in productive activity are at the heart of the definition of the firm. The contractarian view treats the firm as a network of contracts yet focuses almost entirely on the relationship between shareholders and managers. Blair (1999: 58) insists that contractarian views need to recognize that multilateral and multidimensional relationships and agreements among individuals are possible only when it is acknowledged that 'a corporation is a separate entity, and more than the sum of its parts . . . something that cannot protect itself through contract, but that needs to be protected by fiduciary duties and corporation law from possible predatory behaviour by any of the parties'.

The contrast between the absence of a role for workers in Anglo-American interpretations of corporate governance and the increasing role that workers' pension funds have as shareholders is considered by O'Connor (2000), who examines ways of bringing activity around workers' concerns regarding job insecurity, wage inequality, pension fund governance, and investment strategies into closer alignment (Clarke 1978). A different picture of corporate governance in Europe is revealed by Goodijk (2000) who discusses how the Works Council (composed of employees) and Supervisory Board (composed of employee and shareholder representatives) exist and could play a fuller role in strategic decision-making in Dutch companies. European managers have in the past been skilled at stakeholder dialogue as the means to achieve the commitment to change and new strategies; however this could be lost if the newer shareholder-oriented governance models are uncritically accepted. In the context of the continuing changes in corporate governance in Japan, Araki (2005) suggests that although the employee-centred governance model is under threat there from successive waves of new shareholder-oriented governance reforms, there is evidence that what has occurred so far is a realignment of stakeholder interests within an essentially stakeholder model.

7 Globalization and Convergence

7.1 Different Corporate Governance Systems

Different approaches to financing corporations in different regions of the world have prevailed since the diverse origins of capitalism (Hall & Soskice 2001;

Amable 2003; Deeg & Jackson 2007). The evolution of the corporate form can be traced from the family and closely held capitalism of the early nineteenth century with the protection of ownership rights; through to the managerial capitalism of the early twentieth century with further protection for listed corporations and limited liability; and finally, to the popular capitalism of the late twentieth century with protection of minority interests and mass ownership. However, different routes were followed in this evolution and different destinations reached in corporate practice, company law, and associated institutional development of Anglo-American, European, and Asian forms of corporate enterprise. In the Asian system of corporate governance, stronger elements of family ownership survive intact, and in the European system more managerial forms have survived.

7.2 Convergence or Parallel Universes?

The result is two parallel universes of corporate governance: a dispersed ownership model characterized by strong and liquid securities markets, high disclosure standards, high market transparency, and where the market for corporate control is the ultimate disciplining mechanism; and secondly a concentrated ownership model characterized by controlling shareholders, weak securities markets, low transparency and disclosure standards and often a central monitoring role for large banks who have a stake in the company (Coffee 2000; Clarke 2005). The dispersed ownership (market-based, Anglo-American corporate governance systems) and the concentrated ownership (European and Asian relationship based corporate governance systems) are described by a variety of names that reflect their different characteristics: including market systems and block-holder systems, rules-based and relationship-based systems, and market and bank based systems. However, the simplest characterization is that between outsider and insider-based systems.

Outsider systems are typified by dispersed ownership, a clear separation of ownership and control, lower debt/equity ratios, and sophisticated financial markets. In this system, there is less incentive for outsiders to participate in the control of the corporation, except insofar as they do so through the equity markets, and the severest sanction is hostile takeover. The interests of outside stakeholders are not formally represented, and investors themselves often have less interest in the strategic goals of the enterprise than in the short-term returns that are available. In contrast, insider systems are typified by highly concentrated ownership which is closely connected with the managerial control of the enterprise, and high debt/equity ratios, with a higher rate of bank credits due to the closer relationship with banks that are often represented on the board of major corporations along with other stakeholders including related firms and employees. In these systems hostile takeovers rarely, if ever, occur and there is often a dense network of supportive relationships with related businesses that occasionally can develop into collusion.

Intense debate over recent decades has concerned the relative merits of the different corporate governance systems, often with the assumption that the Anglo-American system, with stronger security markets and higher levels of disclosure, represents a more advanced and efficient mode of corporate finance and governance, and leading to the conclusion that inevitably there will be either an early, or more gradual, shift of the European and Asian systems of corporate governance towards the Anglo-American model (Hansmann & Kraakerman 2001; McCahery et al. 2002; Hamilton & Quinlan 2005). However, the argument for inevitable convergence has tended to underestimate the extent of the different orientations and objectives of the alternative systems and the different institutional complementarities that have evolved, and failed to appreciate the significance of different cultures and conceptions of what a company is (McDonnell 2002; Clarke 2017). In different regions of the world there are deeply embedded differences regarding business values and ways of doing things, and very different relationships with stakeholders. There exist profoundly contrasting beliefs in the role of the market in the different systems, which influence the way the corporation is considered: simply as a bundle of tradable assets in the worst-case scenario of the market-based system; but as a productive institution to be passed on to future generations in the best-case of the insider governance system. As a result, different measures of performance are applied, with the market-based system looking for short-term returns, and the European and Japanese systems having much longer-term horizons.

As a consequence of the differences in corporate governance structure and objectives, the different systems demonstrate unique strengths and weaknesses: essentially, they are good at doing different things, and they all have weaknesses (Moerland 1995; Dore et al. 2002). The Anglo-American governance system supports a dynamic market orientation, with fluid capital which can quickly chase market opportunities wherever they occur. This agility and speed equipped the United States to capitalize on the new economy of electronics, software, media, financial, and professional services: an industrial resurgence that reasserted the US global economic ascendancy. The downside of this system is the corollary of its strength: the inherent volatility, short termism, and inadequate governance procedures that often stranded the US manufacturing industry and caused periodic stock market panics and occasional crashes that left the least well-informed investors with crippling losses (Clarke 2017).

A weaker and often disoriented public sector was another casualty of Anglo-American governance (Clarke & Pitelis 2005).

In marked contrast, European enterprise as typified by the German governance system traditionally has committed to a long-term industrial strategy supported by stable capital investment and robust governance procedures that build enduring relationships with key stakeholders (Clarke & Bostock 1997; Cernat 2004; Lane 2003). This was the foundation of the German economic miracle which carried the country forward to becoming the leading exporter in the world of products renowned for their quality and reliability including luxury automobiles, precision instruments, chemicals, and electrical engineering. Again, the weaknesses of the German system were the corollary of its strengths: the depth of relationships leading to a lack of flexibility, that made it difficult to pursue initiatives for new businesses and industries while accumulating costs in established companies, resulting in high unemployment. The Latin variant of European corporate governance as practiced in France and Italy is highly network oriented, with dominant holdings by the state, families, or industrial groups. Ownership concentration provides for stability and long-term horizons, with strong relationships with stakeholders. This governance system has allowed the southern European countries to specialize and enhance their skills in selected industries with notable success, for example in France aerospace and luxury goods, and in Italy fashion and design goods (Goyer 2001). However, in southern Europe often weak governance accountability and frequent network and pyramid control diminishes the integrity of the equity market – the strength of the block-holder relationships precluding others from becoming involved.

Finally, the Asian corporate governance system is the most network based of all, with the firm as the institutional centre of long enduring and deep economic relationships of investors, employees, suppliers, and customers (Claessens & Fan 2002). In the Japanese system, there is a close dependence on bank finance and insider control. This approach has yielded the longest investment horizons of all and was the key to the Japanese success in progressively dominating overseas markets in the US and Europe in electronic consumer goods and automobiles. The Japanese economic miracle came to an abrupt end when paying the price for its own success: the hugely speculative bubble burst in the early 1990s, the resulting decades-long disorientation revealing the weaknesses of secretive and unaccountable Japanese governance. However, the rest of the Asia Pacific is increasingly emulating the success of the Japanese in pursuing innovation in a knowledge economy. The centre of gravity of world manufacturing has moved East, while there remain doubts regarding the strength of governance institutions there to sustain progress (Yoshikawa 2018; Clarke & Lee 2018).

7.3 Globalization of Corporate Governance

The current phase of globalization represents a profound reconfiguration of the world economy compared to earlier periods of internationalization. 'An international economy links distinct national markets; a global economy fuses national markets into a coherent whole' (Kobrin 2002: 7). Early civilizations traded goods and services across vast regions, often forcefully, and more recently internationalization was formalized with the seizure of the colonies, reaching a high-water mark in the years before the First World War (Petrella 1996: 63; Hirst & Thompson 1996: 2). After the dislocation and protectionism resulting from two world wars, the recovery and resurgence of international trade and foreign direct investment from the 1950s was fuelled by the growth of multinational firms involving the transfer of capital and production overseas. The impact of the multinational corporations, as they have driven the process of globalization, has proved substantial and pervasive, and the activities of these imposing corporations developing vast global value chains have become synonymous with the phenomenon of globalization itself.

As the growth of foreign direct investment exceeded the growth in world trade, the centrality of corporations' internationalization strategies to the evolving pattern of the industrial and investment processes of globalization became increasingly apparent, as the OECD acknowledged:

> Globalization of industry refers to an evolving pattern of cross-border activities of firms involving international investment, trade and collaboration for purposes of product development, production and sourcing, and marketing. These international activities enable firms to enter new markets, exploit their technological and organizational advantages, and reduce business costs and risks. Underlying the international expansion of firms, and in part driven by it, are technological advances, the liberalization of markets and increased mobility of production factors. These complex patterns of cross-border activities increasingly characterise the international economic system and distinguish it from the earlier predominance of arms-length trade in finished goods. (OECD 1996: 9)

Different corporate governance systems perform these duties in the context of the enveloping challenges of competitive globalization. There are many interrelationships between the strengths and weaknesses of different approaches to corporate governance and the ensuing achievements and problems of globalization. If multinational corporations can identify with their contribution to the expansion of the global economy, they have to recognize in turn their involvement in the wider dilemmas and tragedies of globalization. The fact that globalization has become one of the most contested concepts in history is due to fundamental disagreements concerning the perception of the interests globalization primarily serves, the processes involved, and the consequences that result.

The key characteristics of globalization contributing to this unequal transformation of the world economy include the liberalization of international trade; expansion of foreign direct investment; emergence of massive cross-border financial flows; increased competition in global markets; policy decisions to reduce national barriers to international economic transactions; impact of new technology, especially in the sphere of information and communications; the acceleration of global environmental degradation; and the social impact of globalization in compounding inequality. It is when these economic, finance, technology, environmental, and social conditions are taken together that the combustible elements of contemporary globalization are fully realized:

> The effects of the new technology have given a distinctive character to the current process of globalization, as compared to similar episodes in the past. The natural barriers of time and space have been vastly reduced. The cost of moving information, people, goods, and capital across the globe has fallen dramatically, while global communication is cheap and instantaneous and becoming ever more so. This has vastly expanded the feasibility of economic transactions across the world. Markets can now be global in scope and encompass an expanding range of goods and services. (World Commission 2004: 24)

7.4 Technological Transformation

The advance of global production, networking, and communicating technologies has been critical to the task of pushing forward economic and financial global integration. These three related and interwoven technological characteristics of the emerging global economy make domestic markets and governance problematic. The scale of technology in many strategic industries (its cost, risk, and complexity) renders the minimal effective market size to achieve a return on investment larger than that of even the largest national markets, pressing corporations to expand their activities overseas. Networks are replacing hierarchies and markets as a basic form of economic organization. The distributed and relational character of networks is not consistent with economic authority exercised through bounded and discrete geographic territory. The migration of markets and economic activity to cyberspace (or some combination of physical and virtual space) renders geographic space problematic as a basis for effective economic governance (Kobrin 2002: 2). Despite the recent dematerialization of much productive activity and its relocation to cyberspace, the cumulative effect of advancing globalization on the physical environment also has to be reckoned with.

7.5 The Impact of Multinational Enterprises

If nation states were written out of the script of globalization far too early, the other great players in the globalization saga are the multinational enterprises that are often assumed to be in the lead role. This view is encouraged by the prominence multinational enterprises now enjoy in the public consciousness, largely due to the vast sums spent on advertising and marketing their brand images. Disparaging comparisons are often made between the rapidly growing revenues and market capitalization of multinational enterprises, and the more halting growth of the economies of many nation states, with the implication that the largest global corporations are becoming more significant economic entities than most nation states.

The autonomy and power of multinational enterprises relative to nation states has often been subject to some exaggeration, however there is much evidence to justify the increasing economic significance of multinational enterprises, and as Calder and Culverwell (2005: 16) argue, the increasing involvement of these corporations in the economies of developing countries is one of the main concerns in recent globalization debates. The sales of the largest 100 multinationals increased from $3.2 trillion to $4.8 trillion between 1990 and 2000 (UNCTAD 2002: 90). By 2017 *Fortune* claimed the 500 largest multinational companies were generating $30 trillion in revenues, and $1.9 trillion in profits. Foreign employment by multinational enterprises grew from 24 million people in 1990 to 54 million people in 2001 (UNCTAD 2002: xv). During this period private sector corporations commenced the operation and construction of approximately 2,500 infrastructure projects in developing countries with a total investment of $750 billion (World Bank 2002: 1). More recently, China has responded with a huge geopolitical and economic strategy of its own in the *Belt and Road Initiative*, that seeks to establish infrastructural pathways and industry links with all of South Asia and Western Asia all the way to Eastern Europe (Cai 2017). Whatever economic benefits might flow from these international projects, they are often shrouded in weak governance and accountability, with poor social and environmental outcomes:

> Weak public sector governance in some developing countries has meant that transnational corporations (TNCs) are often operating in areas with far weaker environmental and social standards than those in their 'home' countries, where human rights are being abused and/or where corruption is endemic. These conditions have been seen to create the risk that the activities of TNCs in these countries will lead to negative environmental and/or social impacts and to human rights abuses. (Calder & Culverwell 2005: 16)

There have been a number of initiatives from the UN, World Bank, and OECD to address these issues, including the OECD (2008 and 2018) *Guidelines for Multinational Enterprises* offering detailed guidance on good business conduct regarding human rights, accountability, disclosure, employment, environmental protection, bribery, and taxation. Though these guidelines are a comprehensive statement on internationally agreed principles, they fail to provide sufficient detail on key issues such as the provision of a living wage, human rights, and tax compliance; the guidelines do not directly apply to small and medium sized enterprises; and their applicability to global supply chains is contested (Calder & Culverwell 2005: 46).

7.6 The Global Value Chain

As global corporations have developed, they have transformed their structure and operations immensely, distributing the supply of materials and components, and the assembly of finished products, throughout the emerging economies but with a focus on the Asia Pacific, while retaining firm control of finance, innovation, design, and marketing in their national headquarters (Clarke & Boersma 2019). The implications of the global value chain for corporate governance are profound and multidimensional in terms of control, accountability, and taxation. Paradoxically they have disaggregated their operations while simultaneously centralizing and concentrating their control of essential and high value-added functions. The continuing advance of global value chains as the contemporary mode of production by corporations for an increasing number of goods and services has impacted considerably on the economies and societies of both the developed world and the emerging economies (Gereffi & Sturgeon 2013; Clarke & Boersma 2017).

The OECD suggests the global value chain manifests the increasing fragmentation of production across countries, the specialization of countries in tasks and business functions rather than specific products, and the role of networks of global buyers and global suppliers: 'This international fragmentation of production is a powerful source of increased efficiency and firm competitiveness. Today, more than half of world manufactured imports are intermediate goods (primary goods, parts and components, and semi-finished products), and more than 70 per cent of world services imports are intermediate services' (OECD 2012: 7, 4; OECD 2013).

7.7 Globalization of Capital Markets

Greater still than the impact of the multinational enterprises and the global value chain upon the globalizing economy, has been the explosive growth of

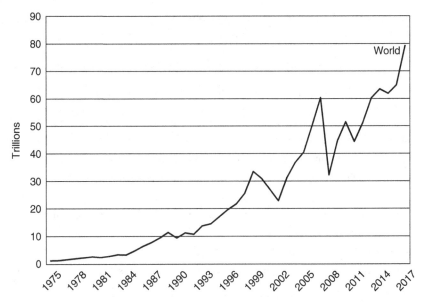

Figure 3 Market Capitalization of Global Listed Domestic Companies
1975–2017
Source: World Bank (2018) https://data.worldbank.org/indicator/CM.MKT.LCAP.CD

the international financial system, which has fuelled the processes of globalization, that have often appeared to dwarf domestic economies. An important
component of this financialization of the world economy is the growth of
capital markets, and the vast growth of equity markets from 1990 to 2018. In
this relatively short period the American zone equity markets (entirely dominated by the NYSE and Nasdaq) were propelled from a total of 4,000 billion
dollars to 40,294 billion dollars in 2018. The European zone markets grew
from just over 2,000 billion dollars in 1990 to 18,815 billion in 2018, while
market capitalization in the Asia Pacific zone grew from just under
4,000 billion in 1990 to 26,395 billion dollars in 2018 (World Federation of
Exchanges 2018a).

The World Bank highlights the exponential growth of the market capitalization of listed corporations reaching nearly US 80 trillion dollars by 2017
(Figure 3). Due to the scale and intensity of the volume of share trading
internationally, the value of global equity trading worldwide far exceeds the
total market capitalization of companies (WFE 2018). Translated into billions
of equity exchange traded derivatives contracts, the hundreds of trillions of
dollars traded on global financial markets ultimately based on listed entities
activity becomes truly startling (WFE 2018). While this is rationalized by
financial institutions as the provision of liquidity and flexibility in capital

markets, it is also a cause of recurrent profound instability in world markets, and ultimately imploding in the global financial crisis of 2007-8.

8 Crisis and Regulation

8.1 Introduction: Cycles of Crisis and Reform

Corporate governance crisis and reform is essentially cyclical (Clarke 2004). Waves of corporate governance reform and increased regulation occur during periods of recession, corporate collapse, and re-examination of the viability of regulatory systems. During long periods of expansion, active interest in governance diminishes, as companies and shareholders become again more concerned with the generation of wealth, than in its retention. This cyclical pattern of stock market booms encouraging and concealing corporate excesses undoubtedly will continue (Clarke 2010).

When crisis and recession highlight corporate failings, statutory intervention invariably occurs. Avoiding mandatory restrictive over-regulation requires active market regulation – particularly in times of expansion. There will never be a 'perfect' system of corporate governance. Market systems are competitive and volatile, and dynamic systems of governance will reflect this. But corporate governance is about risk management. The drive to make corporate governance both improve corporate performance and enhance corporate accountability will continue.

All of the different regional corporate governance systems, even apparently the most successful, have experienced recurrent periods of crisis that have exposed their structural weaknesses. For example, from the 1970s to the present day the World Bank and other international institutions have celebrated the rapid economic growth of the Tiger economies of the Asia Pacific (World Bank 1993 and 2018; Mason & Shetty 2019). Yet, following the 1997-8 Asian financial crisis, the weak finance and governance institutions of the Asia Pacific were highlighted (Clarke 2000). Just as the OECD, World Bank, and IMF were increasingly confidently projecting the Anglo-American market-based outsider system of governance as the pre-eminent model from which all other countries might learn, the Enron disaster occurred. The corrosive greed that became an integral part of the incentive system in US corporate governance yielded a more sinister fruit in the protracted spate of corporate frauds and bankruptcies of 2001-2.

8.2 Enron and WorldCom Bankruptcy and the Collapse of the Nasdaq 2001/2002

Bubbles have permeated stock markets from their beginnings, but the vast scale of unprecedented US stock market bubbles in 2001 and again in 2007 is hard to imagine: 'American stock price behaviour at the turn of the millennium had all the characteristics of a classic bubble: prices climbed much faster than dividends or earnings ... Between January 1980 and August 2000 American stock prices as measured by the S&P 500 index rose by 1239 per cent; over the same period the dividends on the shares underlying the index rose by only 188 per cent, while the earnings rose by 254 per cent' (Brennan 2004: 1). The precipitous rise of share prices was followed by a calamitous fall: 'In the period 2000–2002 the New York market suffered the biggest stock market crash in US history compared with GNP. Since early 2000 when it peaked at $15,000 billion, market capitalisation fell by $7,000 billion, i.e., 46 per cent, and those who invested at the top of the market lost half of their investments' (Taylor 2003: 158; *The Economist*, 7 September 2002).

Leading corporations at the head of the new economy lost more than half their market value during this period including Microsoft, Cisco, and Intel, many smaller new technology companies came close to bankruptcy, and even established corporations such as General Electric and Pfizer lost 40 per cent of their market capitalization (Financial Times 17 November 2005).

The apparently dynamic, competitive, and performance-oriented US economy of the 1990s degenerated over time as executives, faced with the necessity to demonstrate ever increasing returns, resorted to illegal means to do so (Boyer 2005). Creative accounting and a, sometimes criminal, collusion between executives, auditors, and analysts inflated a speculative bubble that finally burst, but not before many executives had cashed in their options, leaving their own employees destitute and superannuation funds depleted around the world. The chairman of the Public Company Accounting Oversight Board, William J. McDonagh, speaking at the Federal Reserve Bank of New York, graphically exposed the causes of the 2001-2 US stock market crash:

For 10 years, the United States enjoyed the longest economic expansion in the country's history. What could go wrong? Morality went wrong. In the mid-1990s, it became fashionable for companies in America to guide allegedly independent investment analysts to a view of the company's forthcoming quarterly earnings. We know that all numbers on a financial statement are estimates, including cash if the company operates in more than one currency. As a result, there is a certain amount of room for those estimates to be shaded to make the forecast. And then it became fashionable to expect and forecast ever-rising earnings, meaning, essentially, that product cycles and unexpected shocks and even the law of gravity no longer applied. It was a formula for cooking the books – and the books got cooked. There was another motive to cook the books. If earnings are good and always moving upward, the equity market loves it, and the stock multiple improves. That is really great if you are a senior executive, and your remuneration is related to the stock price. And that was the case. In 1993, the US Congress passed a law limiting the expensing for tax purposes of the remuneration of any individual to $1 million per year, unless that remuneration is incentive-based. That law was the fairy godmother of stock options, which of course are incentive-based. And total remuneration grew spectacularly: in 1980, the average CEO of a Fortune 500 company made 40 times more than the average employee of the company. By 2000, that multiple had leaped by a factor of 10 to 400 times. I find it grotesquely immoral – explainable by no economic theory or principle other than greed. (2005: 1)

8.3 International Weaknesses in Governance

While the cyclical nature of market booms and busts is much more pronounced in the Anglo-American system of finance and governance, there are weaknesses in governance throughout the world. Both the European and Asian forms of corporate governance have experienced some acute difficulties. Though Europeans have not witnessed anything quite as catastrophic as the corporate collapses in the US, there have periodically been disasters, for example the Parmalat debacle which revealed a leading Italian listed company had been used as personal property by its chief executive for many years, without detection or accountability. There are continuing doubts concerning the close network relationships that did typify much of European enterprise, and that often still exist (IFC 2015; Clarke & Chanlat 2009).

In the Asia Pacific the miracle tiger economies stalled in the Asian Financial Crisis of 1997-8 in which a speculative frenzy, with inadequate financial controls, led to the collapse of stock markets, currencies, and financial institutions (Clarke 2000). Though an export-led recovery rescued the growth of the East Asian economies, systemic weaknesses remained apparent in Asian modes of governance, where the separation of ownership and control has not taken hold:

> In all East Asian countries control is enhanced through pyramid structures and cross-holdings, among firms. Voting rights consequently exceed formal cash flow rights, especially in Indonesia, Japan, and Singapore. We find that more than two-thirds of firms are controlled by a single shareholder. Separation of management from ownership control is rare, and the top management of about 60 per cent of firms that are not widely held is related to the family of controlling shareholder. (Claessens et al. 2000: 82)

Empirical research by Claessens et al. 2000) revealed countries in Asia with a higher concentration of ownership of companies among a few families or block-holders showed the least progress in adopting institutional reforms. Hence insider-controlled companies are frequently associated with a neglect of minority shareholder rights, as legal and judicial systems were not developed or active, and widespread corruption was often tolerated (as illustrated in even the most successful economies of Asia, as in recent scandals at Samsung in Korea, and Nissan and Olympus in Japan). After a long passage of reforms over two decades, there is greater proficiency in the fundamentals of corporate governance in many countries of Asia (OECD 2017a), however in China the urge to adopt international standards of accountability has been tempered by the universal presence of state and party influence (ACGA 2018). These insecure and unstable political, financial, and governance institutions could prove the cause of further crises in future.

8.4 The Global Financial Crisis 2007/2008

The global financial crisis exposed the deepening instability of Anglo-American economies, and how recurrent crises are connected to profound structural and institutional weaknesses in the system. The US Federal Reserve under Alan Greenspan had responded to the collapse of confidence caused by the Nasdaq disaster and Enron/WorldCom failures in 2001-2 by reducing US interest rates to 1 per cent, their lowest in 45 years, flooding the market with cheap credit to jump-start the economy back into life. US business did recover faster than expected, but the cheap credit had washed into the financial services and housing sectors, producing the largest speculative bubbles ever witnessed in the American economy (Fleckenstein 2008). The scene was set by the 1999 dismantling of the 1932 Glass–Steagall Act which had separated commercial banking from investment banking and insurance services, opening the way for a consolidation of the vastly expanding and increasingly competitive US financial services industry. Phillips (2008: 5) describes this as a 'burgeoning debt and credit complex,' both volatile and dangerous.

As the new financial derivatives were developed and marketed, the securities markets grew massively in the 2000s, dwarfing the growth of the real economy. For example, according to the Bank of International Settlements, the global derivatives markets grew at the rate of 32 per cent per annum from 1990, and the notional amount of derivatives reached $106 trillion by 2002, $477 trillion by 2006, and over $531 trillion by 2008 (though gross market value is a small fraction of this) (McKinsey & Company 2008: 20). The supposed purpose of this increasingly massive exercise was to hedge risk and add liquidity to the financial system.

The prolonged systemic crisis in international financial markets commencing in 2007 was also a crisis in corporate governance and regulation. The apparent ascendancy of Anglo-American markets and governance institutions was profoundly questioned by the scale and contagion of the global financial crisis.

Instead of risk being hedged, it had become interconnected, international, and unknown. The market capitalization of the stock markets of the world had peaked at $62 trillion at the end of 2007. By October 2008 they were in free fall, having lost $33 trillion, over half of their value, in 12 months of unrelenting financial and corporate failures, climaxing in the collapse of Lehman Brothers, the largest bankruptcy in history (Clarke 2020).

The most severe financial disaster since the Great Depression of the 1930s exposed the dangers of unregulated financial markets and nominal corporate governance. The crisis originated in Wall Street, where deregulation unleashed highly incentivized investment banks to flood world markets with toxic financial products. As a stunning series of banks and investment companies collapsed in the US and then in Europe, a frightening dimension of the global economy became fully apparent: a new world disorder of violently volatile markets and deep financial insecurity (Clarke & Chanlat 2009; Clarke 2014b). The apparent ascendancy of Anglo-American markets and governance institutions was profoundly questioned by the scale and contagion of the 2008 global financial crisis, as Joseph Stiglitz (2008: 37) stated: 'America's financial institutions have not managed risk; they have created it.'

8.5 Post-crisis Reform of Corporate Governance

The worldwide commitment towards improving standards of corporate governance has encompassed a succession of legislative changes to company law, beginning with the Sarbanes-Oxley Act 2002 in the US, and progressive legal reform has occurred in almost all jurisdictions. This has been supported by the national corporate governance codes introduced in many countries. Reinforcing the effort to achieve substantial reform, the international agencies – especially the OECD, World Bank, and Asian Development Bank – have maintained a constant drive towards the adoption of more rules-based corporate governance systems. This culminated in the publication of the OECD *Principles of Corporate Governance* in 1999, revised in 2004 in the light of the post-Enron lessons, and later further revised with the support of the G20 in 2015 following the global financial crisis. A growing number of corporate governance ratings agencies have monitored changes at both corporate and national levels (OECD 2017b).

However diligent the process of corporate governance reform was in the Anglo-American economies in the post-Enron period of 2002–7, and whatever the respective merits of the US black letter law approach as in Sarbanes–Oxley or the principles-based approach as in the UK Combined Code, nothing prepared the US or UK regulators, boards, lawyers, accountants, or executives themselves for the sudden and dramatic onslaught of the global financial crisis. This crisis exposed critical and dangerous weaknesses in Anglo-American regulation, governance, and risk management and brought the international economy teetering to the brink of complete collapse.

While the accumulated vast cost of the global financial crisis was being realized, the commitment to establish a new international financial regulatory framework increased (Clarke & Klettner 2011). The costs of all forms of intervention to alleviate the crisis by the US government ballooned out to $7.7 trillion. These costs included credit discounts, credit extensions, securities lending, term auction facilities, portfolio funding, money market funding, the Troubled Asset Relief Program (TARP), assistance to specific institutions, economic stimulus packages, and homeowner assistance. The general market assistance and specific rescue packages for individual financial institutions amounted to over $10 trillion worldwide by October 2008. Though these funds could be regarded as a temporary investment in the financial economy, with the hope of recouping most of the funds back at a later stage, this was an optimistic view when the crisis spread to other sectors of the economy.

There was a widespread sense that this regulatory failure of financial markets could not be allowed to occur again. A problem in devising a new financial regulatory architecture was that Bretton Woods in 1944, though it established the International Monetary Fund and World Bank, was essentially dealing with national financial markets. Digital and interconnected global financial markets presented a much bigger challenge. The International Basel Committee on Banking Supervision (BCBS) was tasked with the job of translating the reform principles of the G20 into a regulatory architecture that might transform the international financial system. This culminated in 'Basel III', a comprehensive set of reform measures, developed by the BCBS to strengthen the regulation, supervision, and risk management of the banking sector. These measures were aimed to:

• improve the banking sector's ability to absorb shocks arising from financial and economic stress, whatever the source;
• improve risk management and governance; and
• strengthen banks' transparency and disclosures.

This reform effort is substantial and real, and when the Basel III guidelines were released in 2010 there was great expectation regarding their implementation in 2013. However, over time this commitment has diminished as business-as-usual practices are reasserted. The lobbyists for US banks asserted that their institutions were already raising their holdings of liquid assets, and implementation timelines were relaxed, meaning that final global implementation only occurred fully by 2019. Critics are concerned that there is no restraint on banks to hold capital against some high-risk assets, and though it may be more costly for banks to engage in high-risk behaviour, they are still able to this.

If the delay in the implementation of the Basel III reforms was disappointing, the protracted stripping away of the legislative intent and regulatory traction of the Dodd–Frank Act is a much greater tragedy. After prolonged legislative battles, the *Dodd–Frank Wall Street Reform and Consumer Protection Act* was finally passed by the Obama administration in 2010, as a bulwark against the excesses that led to the global financial crisis. The question arises whether this massive swathe of legislation, however well intentioned, once denuded of much of the intended impact by the well-funded Wall Street lobbyists in Washington, will have the intended effect. The global financial crisis and its aftermath consisted of multiple and compounding failures in financial markets, institutions, regulation, and governance. The 'animal spirits' unleashed in unfettered securities markets, massive incentivization of risk-taking and leverage, and the abandonment of effective governance and ethical commitments occurred in a regulatory vacuum (Akerlof & Shiller 2009). Governments were convinced that lightening the burden of regulation was the means to promote more dynamic financial markets and business development. The realization of the consequences of unchecked systemic risks has prompted national governments and international agencies into a major series of regulatory reforms and interventions in financial markets and institutions, the effect of which remains to be discerned.

The Wall Street banks are now larger and more remote than before, continue business as usual, and have not fundamentally changed their behaviour, leading Elizabeth Warren, the campaigning US Senator, to call for a twenty-first century Glass–Steagall Act, to 'ensure they [the banks] are not too big to fail – or, for that matter, too big to manage, too big to regulate, too big for trial, or too big for jail' (Warren 2017).

There is a profound paradox that after two decades of corporate governance reform, governments and corporations remain fully engaged in the governance challenges posed by the transformation of markets, operations, and technologies in the finance sector. As one authority stated: 'We have not yet fully understood the causes of the last financial crisis and have not begun to prepare for the next one.'

The belief that the considerable efforts by government to rescue and reform financial institutions and markets would lead to sustained stability and security in the sector was rudely dispelled in a prolonged sequence of bank scandals and market failures in the years following the financial crisis. The banking crisis segued into a sovereign debt crisis in southern Europe, with governments facing challenges in funding their activities. This was quickly followed by seismic eruptions in the mainstream financial institutions with the revelations surrounding the London Interbank Offered Rate (LIBOR) rate fixing. A total of $10 trillion in loans and $350 trillion in derivatives worldwide were indexed to LIBOR. As the US Financial Stability Oversight Council (established by the Dodd–Frank Act to identify risks to financial stability, promote market discipline, and respond to emerging threats) highlighted:

> Recent investigations uncovered systemic false reporting and manipulations of reference rate submissions dating back many years. This misconduct was designed to either increase the potential profit of the submitting firms or to convey a misleading picture of the relative health of the submitting banks. These actions were pervasive, occurred in multiple bank locations around the world, involved senior bank officials at several banks, and affected multiple benchmark rates and currencies, including LIBOR, EURIBOR, and the Tokyo Interbank Offered Rate (TIBOR). Each of the banks that faced charges engaged in a multi-year pattern of misconduct that involved collusion with other banks. (FSOC 2013: 137)

This rate manipulation predated the 2008 financial crisis and had continued long after the government support and intervention in the banking sector following the financial crisis, revealing how constricted any ostensible change in governance and ethics within the banks actually was. After a major inquiry into Barclays' involvement in the LIBOR rate-rigging, and subpoenas to JP Morgan, Deutsche Bank, Royal Bank of Scotland Group, HSBC, Citigroup, and UBS, all of the banks settled for fines amounting to billions of dollars with the Department of Justice and Commodities Futures Trading Commission (CFTC) in the United States, and the Financial Services Authority (FSA) in the United Kingdom.

9 Corporate Responsibility and Corporate Sustainability

9.1 The Licence to Operate

Since the origins of industrial capitalism, corporations have wrestled with the dilemma of whether their sole purpose is to generate wealth (narrowly defined as financial profit) or whether corporations have broader obligations to the communities in which they are situated, and from which they derive not only their fundamental resources (employees, materials, customers) but their *licence to operate* – that is, their legitimacy. Bridging the divide between corporate governance and corporate social responsibility has proved a great challenge to managers for generations (Benn & Dunphy 2007; Clarke 2015a).

Increasingly today the social and environmental impact of the corporation will be assessed in deciding whether the corporation is viable or not, by governments, regulators, investors, and other stakeholders, even if the corporations' management are reluctant themselves to make this assessment. The licence to operate can no longer be readily assumed for any corporation, and in an increasing number of economic, industrial, and social contexts needs to be earned with verifiable evidence of the social and environmental responsibility of the corporation (Clarke 2015b).

9.2 Defining Corporate Social Responsibility

Definitions of CSR and sustainability have evolved over time and range from the basic to the most demanding, from a specific reference to a number of necessary activities to demonstrate responsibility, to a general call for a comprehensive, integrated, and committed pursuit of social and environmental sustainability (Crane et al. 2014; Klettner et al. 2014). 'There is a massive problem around terminology,' argues Jane Nelson (EIU 2008a: 6), director of the Corporate Social Responsibility Initiative at Harvard University. Even when two companies use the same term, 'one of them might be looking at corporate responsibility much more from a supply-chain management, managing risks, human rights perspective' whereas another might be thinking, 'how do we make money out of this?'" (EIU 2008a: 6). Undoubtedly CSR has matured over recent decades, driven by evolving global guidelines, national regulations, increased stakeholder expectations, and more demanding corporate disclosure requirements, together with widespread voluntary initiatives by corporations to embed CSR into their core business. Yet as Jane Nelson insists, what is presently happening lacks the speed and scale to bring about the systemic change required to remedy increasing social and environmental dilemmas:

> The negative headlines persist, fuelled by reports of sweat-shops in low-income countries producing cheap goods for OECD markets, fatal tragedies such as the collapse of the Rana Plaza garment factory in Bangladesh in 2013 and the Turkish mining disaster in 2014, and catastrophic environmental accidents. Moreover, the legacy of the global financial crisis, concerns about corporate tax practices, and challenges such as youth unemployment and climate change have forced corporations to lift their sights further above the bottom line and to judge their performance against wider social goals. (Nelson 2014)

The following are some definitions of corporate social responsibility, each of which have different emphases:

- The integration of stakeholders' social, environmental and other concerns into a company's business operations (EIU 2005: 2).
- The commitment of businesses to contribute to sustainable economic development by working with their employees, their families, the local community,

and society at large to improve their lives in ways which are good for business and for development (World Business Council for Sustainable Development 2002).

• Corporate social responsibility being, at heart, a process of managing the costs and benefits of business activity to both internal (for example, workers, shareholders, investors) and external (institutions of public governance, community members, civil society groups, other enterprises) stakeholders. Setting the boundaries for how those costs and benefits are managed is partly a question of business policy and strategy and partly a question of public governance (World Bank 2002a: 1).

Sustainability as a whole (planet, environment, species) is an altogether more ambitious project with more expansive definitions than CSR, as sustainability is focused on more fundamental problems. 'All economic activity occurs in the natural, physical world. Economic activities require resources such as energy, materials, and land. Further, economic activity invariably generates material residuals, which enter the environment as waste or polluting emissions. The Earth, being a finite planet, has a limited capability to supply resources and to absorb pollution' (UNEP 2010:9). Corporations have a vital role to play in this fundamental sustainability also, beginning with a modest recognition of their necessary subordination to the interests of maintaining a balanced ecosystem

To help clarify the different approaches to corporate social responsibility, Garriga & Mele (2004) attempt a classification of the main theories and related approaches into four groups: *instrumental* theories, in which the corporation is seen as simply an instrument for wealth creation, and its social activities are only a means to achieve economic results; *political* theories, concerned with the power of corporations in society and the responsible use of this power in the political arena; *integrative* theories, concerned with the corporation's responsibility to meet social demands; and *ethical* theories, based on ethical responsibilities of corporations to society. These theories represent four dimensions of corporate activity related to profits, political performance, social demands, and ethical values. How to balance and integrate these four dimensions remains a vital task in resolving the relationship of business and society.

It is clear that corporations are now facing an imperative to act more responsibly. Many large international corporations have responded to this imperative with well formulated, and often well-orchestrated initiatives on demonstrating their commitment to social and environmental responsibility. However, questions are often addressed concerning the sincerity of corporate social and environmental initiatives; the legality of company directors engaging in these concerns; the legality of the trustees of investment institutions attending to these interests; and the verifiability of CSR activities and outcomes.

9.3 The Impact of Corporate Social Responsibility

The narrow focus of corporate governance exclusively upon the internal control of the firm and simply complying with regulation is no longer tenable. In the past this has allowed corporations to act in extremely irresponsible ways by externalizing social and environmental costs. In the name of normal business activity, corporations were too often given a licence to destroy people's lives and damage the environment.

> Just as evolution has made the shark a perfect eating machine, the device of limited liability has allowed the corporation to perfect its function ... The function perfected by limited liability is that of permitting corporations to externalize the costs of stock price maximisation, that is to push those costs onto others. The corporation is the perfect externalizing machine (Mitchell 2001: 2).

Corporate objectives described as 'wealth generating' too frequently have resulted in a tragic loss of well-being to communities and the ecology. But increasingly in the future the licence to operate will not be given so readily to corporations and other entities (Clarke 2019a). A licence to operate will depend on maintaining the highest standards of integrity and practice in corporate behaviour. Corporate governance essentially will involve a sustained and responsible monitoring of not just the financial health of the company, but also the social and environmental impact of the company.

Explaining the paradox that it is those industries and businesses that are often considered the most irresponsible and damaging to people and the environment that have often apparently been at the forefront of the CSR movement, Crane et al. (2014a: 3) argue:

> Corporations are clearly taking up this challenge. This began with "the usual suspects" such as companies in the oil, chemical and tobacco industries. As a result of media pressure, major disasters, and sometimes government regulation, these companies realized that propping up oppressive regimes, being implicated in human rights violations, polluting the environment, or misinforming and deliberately harming their customers, just to give a few examples, were practices that had to be reconsidered if they wanted to survive and prosper.

Today, however, virtually all businesses, industries, and markets are experiencing increasing demands to legitimate their practices. For example, banking, retailing, tourism, food and beverages, entertainment, and healthcare industries, once considered comparatively responsible and 'clean' industries, are now revealed to have potentially harmful impacts socially and environmentally and are coming under insistent pressure to apply more responsible practices (Crane et al. 2014: 3–4).

A substantial increase in the range, significance, and impact of corporate social and environmental initiatives in recent years suggests the growing materiality of sustainability. Once regarded as a concern of a few philanthropic individuals and companies, corporate social and environmental responsibility appears to be becoming established in many corporations as a critical element of strategic direction, and one of the main drivers of business development, as well as an essential component of risk management. The relationship between corporate governance mechanisms and corporate social responsibility remains complex, with a contested interface (Jain & Jamali 2016). Yet, corporate social and environmental responsibility seems to be rapidly moving from the margins to the mainstream of corporate activity, with greater recognition of a direct and inescapable relationship between corporate governance, corporate responsibility, and sustainable development. The burgeoning importance of this newly revived movement is demonstrated by the current frequency and scale of CSR activity at every level (Calder & Culverwell 2005: 43).

9.4 Multilateral Initiatives on Corporate Social Responsibility

A growing number of international agencies are committed campaigners for corporate social and environmental responsibility, led by the United Nations, ILO, and World Bank. The OECD (2009) also is active in the promotion of corporate social responsibility in its guidelines for the operations of multinational corporations; and the European Union is directly encouraging corporate social responsibility as the business contribution to sustainable development (OECD 2001b; European Commission 2014a). The European Commission calls on European enterprises to strive to comply with and act in accordance with internationally recognized CSR guidelines and principles, such as the:

- OECD *Guidelines for Multinational Enterprises* (2008; 2018);
- 10 principles of the UN *Global Compact* (2013);
- UN *Guiding Principles on Business and Human Rights* (2011);
- ILO Tri-partite *Declaration of Principles on Multinational Enterprises and Social Policy* (2017); and
- ISO 26000 Guidance Standard on Social Responsibility (2010) (European Commission 2014a).

At the national level, a growing number of governments in Europe, and across the globe, have identified strongly with the call for corporate social and environmental responsibility, even with the evident difficulties in applying successive UN international agreements on emissions reductions and creating an effective international climate policy regime. The UNEP (2019xx) review of climate change concludes: 'Decarbonizing the global economy will require fundamental structural changes, which should be designed to bring multiple co-benefits for humanity and planetary support systems.'

The growing body of international policy on corporate responsibility includes much on why companies should voluntarily adopt a responsible approach to business but little on how this might be achieved in practice (Lindgreen & Swaen 2010; Yuan et al. 2011: 76). Partly this is due to the difficulty in defining corporate responsibility in practice – its meaning can be different depending on a company's size, industry, and location. Ultimately, every company has to develop a CSR strategy tailored to both internal and external contingencies which will be unique to the company concerned: 'It is important to reemphasize that corporate sustainability is fundamentally a complex problem and there are no approaches that universally apply. Corporations are faced with differing stakeholder demands, continually shifting priorities, and a multitude of alternatives to address their sustainability challenges' (Searcy 2012: 250).

Yet with the development and widespread voluntary uptake of international standards and frameworks for corporate responsibility such as the United Nations *Global Compact* (UNGC) and the Global Reporting Initiative (GRI), research into effective implementation is becoming important (Baumann and Scherer 2010; Schembera 2012). These instruments provide broad principles and reporting frameworks but leave it to the companies to decide how to implement these principles. The GRI has been adopted worldwide as a means of integrated reporting. Together with many other international, national, and private sector initiatives, the knowledge and practice of sustainability and corporate social responsibility has gained global significance. However, the proliferating range of sustainability standards and initiatives itself poses challenges even for corporations committed to performing well:

> The current CSR landscape is complex and multi-faceted. There are now literally hundreds of private initiatives, often with their own code or set of standards and principles which offer guidance on social and environmental issues. Their focus, membership, usage, and structures vary widely. In the main, they share a desire to help enhance the contribution that business organizations can make to improvement of social and environmental conditions, including labour and other human rights. Since existing instruments evolve and new ones are emerging, a comprehensive yet accessible listing is

almost impossible. In this complex universe there are two foremost international instruments relevant to CSR – the ILO *Declaration* and the OECD *Guidelines* – and one important international CSR initiative – the UN *Global Compact* (UNGC) – which have either been developed and formally agreed by governments or received high-level recognition by governments at an international level. Indeed, the standards and principles set out in the ILO *Declaration*, the OECD *Guidelines*, and the UNGC are universal and derive directly from international normative frameworks. The ILO *Declaration* and the OECD *Guidelines* provide detailed recommendations on responsible business conduct, while helping businesses and stakeholders distinguish between the responsibility of enterprises and that of the state. The UNGC provides a high profile means for mobilizing and encouraging enterprises to integrate CSR into their daily operations. (OECD 2009: 237)

Integrative work on combining the strengths of the central international CSR and sustainability initiatives and making frameworks more compatible and coherent was progressed (GRI 2015). Paul Hohnen participated in the development of the ISO 26000 standard, contributed to the updated OECD *Guidelines*, and was a Strategy Director of the GRI, and has helped provide useful integrative tools (GRI 2011a, 2011b). Sustainability is receiving considerably increased attention internationally, and the material link with economic, social, and environmental benefits is becoming increasingly appreciated.

9.5 Symbolic or Substantive Corporate Social Responsibility?

Nevertheless, there is a need for better understanding of exactly what companies are doing in the absence of clear practical guidance. Are these frameworks simply being used as window dressing, or are they motivating real change? Is there a need for governments to take a more active role in guiding corporate practice? In examining the response of managers to shareholder activism, David et al. concluded that their results were 'consistent with other research which indicates managers may opt for symbolic, rather than substantive, responses to external pressures' (2007: 98). For example, when it comes to environmental performance, Berrone and Gomez Mejia point out that it might be easier for a company to set up a board environment committee than to actually reduce or eliminate toxic emissions (2009: 120).

Whitehouse is also sceptical, pointing out the obvious gap between the seemingly enthusiastic adoption of CSR by companies and the ambiguous nature of the concept: 'This ability to implement policies founded upon a concept that remains ambiguous raises a number of questions regarding the definition employed by those who profess a commitment to CSR, why they have chosen to implement CSR policies, how they develop those policies, and their value in terms of reducing the adverse impact of corporate activity' (2006: 280).

At the corporate level, the World Business Council for Sustainable Development and the World Economic Forum Global Corporate Citizenship Initiative have projected corporate responsibility in the minds of the international business elite (WBCSD 2014 and 2015; WEF 2012). Other business organizations active in promoting CSR include the Business Leaders' Initiative on Human Rights, the Conference Board, Business in the Community, and Business for Social Responsibility. A large number of leading corporations have signed up for the Global Reporting Initiative, and more than 2,000 international corporations now publish reports on their CSR performance (many accessible on www.csrwire.com) (GRI 2015a). Reinforcing the newfound willingness on the part of corporate executives to disclose their commitments to CSR are the new indices, including the Dow Jones Sustainability Index and FTSE4Good. Finally, there are a proliferating number of consultancies, NGOs, and campaign groups offering guidance and actively monitoring CSR activities along the entire length of the global value chain (World Bank 2016).

9.6 The Integrity of Corporate Social Responsibility

Despite the recent burst of enthusiasm for corporate social and environmental responsibility in some quarters, the concept and practice of CSR still provokes a degree of understandable scepticism, partly due to CSR's record of lapsing into amoral apologetics for unacceptable corporate behaviour, and to the apparent capacity of corporations, particularly in the resources sector to express CSR ideals while engaging in every opportunity to make money regardless of the environmental or social consequences (Christian Aid 2004; Corporate Responsibility Coalition 2005; Wright & Nyberg 2015).

David Vogel in a review conducted for the Brookings Institute, *The Market for Virtue: The Potential and Limits of Corporate Social Responsibility* (2005), contends there are many reasons why companies may choose to behave more responsibly in the absence of legal requirements to do so, including strategic, defensive, altruistic, or public-spirited motivations. However, despite pressure from consumers for responsibly made products, the influence of socially responsible investors, and the insistent call for companies to be accountable to a broader community of stakeholders, there are important limits to the market for virtue:

> CSR is best understood as a niche rather than a generic strategy: it makes sense for some firms in some areas under some circumstances. Many of the proponents of corporate social responsibility mistakenly assume that because some companies are behaving more responsibly in some areas, some firms can be expected to behave more responsibly in more areas. This assumption is

misinformed. There is a place in the market economy for responsible firms. But there is also a large place for their less responsible competitors … Precisely because CSR is voluntary and market-driven, companies will engage in CSR only to the extent that it makes business sense for them to do. Civil regulation has proven capable of forcing some companies to internalize some of the negative externalities associated with some of their economic activities. But CSR can reduce only some market failures. (Vogel 2005: 3–4)

Vogel concludes that CSR has a multidimensional nature, and companies, like individuals, do not always exhibit consistent moral or social behaviour, and may behave better in some countries than others depending on the social and environmental policies existing there. Since the origins of capitalism, there have always been more or less responsible firms, and though it may be heartening that executives in many highly visible firms may be becoming more responsive (if only as a result of external stakeholder pressures), the reality is that the amounts wasted on the losses due to financial fraud, and the very substantial – and some would argue unwarranted – increases in executive compensation in corporations in the recent period far exceed any resources companies have devoted to CSR. More worryingly still, the adoption of corporate social responsibility principles by corporations around the world in recent decades seems to have coincided with the largely successful systemic attempt by corporations to avoid public taxation, in the process critically undermining the fiscal basis of social democracy and the welfare state with serious long-term consequences for the communities in which they operate, as public services such as health and education are undermined by lack of funding. This has prompted the European Commission to devise robust rules against tax base erosion and profit shifting by corporations engaged in increasingly aggressive tax avoidance schemes (European Commission 2016).

In a similar vein, Deborah Doane (2005) is sceptical regarding optimism about the power of market mechanisms to deliver social and environmental change, referring to the key myths informing the CSR movement as:

- The market can deliver both short-term financial returns and long-term social benefits;
- The ethical consumer will drive change;
- There will be a competitive 'race to the top' over ethics amongst businesses; and
- In the global economy countries will compete to have the best ethical practices.

In support of her argument that these are largely mythological trends, she highlights the insistence of stock markets upon short-term results, and the failure of companies to invest in long-term benefits; the considerable gap between green consciousness expressed by consumers and their consumer behaviour; the inconsistency between companies' alignment to CSR schemes and their successful efforts to bring about the sustained fall in corporate taxation in the United States and other jurisdictions in recent decades; and finally the evidence emerging in developing countries of governments competing to reduce their insistence on the observance of social and environmental standards to attract international investment (Doane 2005). In a bleak prognosis, Wright and Nyberg (2015) insist corporations are simply obscuring the link between endless economic growth and the ultimate end of the ecology of the planet in a collaborative process of creative self-destruction.

It may well be the case that further significant legislative and regulatory intervention will be required to ensure all corporations fully respond to the growing public demand that they recognize their wider social and environmental responsibilities. However, it is useful to examine how far CSR objectives can be achieved within existing law and regulation. If there is substantial evidence of leading corporations demonstrating it is possible to voluntarily commit to social and environmental performance and to achieve commercial success – perhaps because of, rather than in spite of, ethical commitments – then it will be more straightforward to press for the legislative changes necessary to deal with corporations that refuse to acknowledge their wider responsibilities, as well as finding appropriate legislative support for companies that wish to develop further their CSR commitments.

9.7 The Fragility of the Natural Environment

What is emerging as the most important – and fragile – relationship of all, is that between corporate activity and the ecology. Climate change caused by greenhouse gases, issued largely by the burning of fossil fuels, is endangering the natural environment of the planet. This has become the most critical issue for both corporate governance and corporate social responsibility to address – if corporations and economies are to achieve sustainability, they can only do so through creating a balance with the natural environment (Hawken et al. 1999). The corporate world is a long way from achieving this balance: six of the largest ten corporations in the world by revenue are energy companies firmly based in the fossil fuel sector (Fortune 2018).

Cogan (2006) illuminates in detail the connection between corporate governance and climate change in a comprehensive examination of how the world's largest corporations are positioning themselves in a carbon-constrained world. Investors are increasingly assigning value to companies responding to the business challenges and opportunities posed by climate change and will assign more risk to companies that are slow to do this. Corporate effectiveness in combating climate change will increasingly be measured in terms of board oversight, management execution, public disclosure, emissions accounting, and strategic planning for emissions reduction.

Stern (2006) considers the challenges of building and sustaining frameworks for international collective action on climate change with important initiatives coming from both national governments and corporations. The various dimensions of action required to reduce the risks of climate change are considered: both for mitigation (including through carbon prices and markets, interventions to support low-carbon investment and technology diffusion, cooperation on technology development and deployment, and action to reverse deforestation), and for adaptation. These dimensions of remedial action are interdependent. A carbon price is essential to provide incentives for investment in low-carbon technology around the world, and can be strongly complemented by international cooperation to bring down the costs of new low carbon technologies. The success of international cooperation on mitigation will determine the scale of action required for adaptation, that is, how we learn to cope with climate change. An overview of existing international cooperation on climate change indicates the immense scale of the problem, and the huge global effort that will be required to resolve this. Responsible corporate governance will be essential to securing a sustainable balance between business, society, and the environment.

Corporations have a central role to play in the two main strategies for combating climate change by mitigation and adaptation. Diminishing the potentially catastrophic consequences of the increasing impact of climate change will require urgent efforts to reduce carbon emissions. Corporations are required to make a major contribution to emissions mitigation, and if they refuse to do so will face reputational damage, higher energy costs, legal costs, and fines from increasingly rigorous emissions regulation. More critically, they may find it increasingly difficult to transfer the risk they encounter through insurance, and also discover they are being deserted by investors and credit providers concerned at the exposure to emissions-intensive sectors, stranded assets, and declining industries (Barker et al. 2016; Clarke 2016).

The hazards associated with climate change are both considerable and pervasive and are characterized by their complexity and interconnectedness. The dramatic climactic discontinuities caused by climate change 'may give rise to cascading risks of potentially unforeseeable magnitude' (Godden et al. 2013: 235). Therefore, climate change cannot be framed as one of technical risk management for government and specialists; it is the responsibility of everyone, but particularly those in leadership positions in corporations that have a significant environmental impact.

10 Conclusions

10.1 Fatal Weaknesses in Corporate Governance

The discipline of corporate governance has developed considerably in recent decades. Governments, regulators, and legal and financial institutions have firmly embraced corporate governance as the means to deliver accountability, performance, and integrity. Whether corporate governance in finance, or in any other business sector, can deliver practically and consistently on these essential principles remains open to some speculation. But fatal weaknesses also are becoming more apparent in both the academic analysis of corporate governance and the ensuing policy deliberations:

- Corporate governance has become identified almost exclusively with endless templates for compliance and regulation;
- Corporate governance is overwhelmed by the intellectual constrictions of agency theory (Weinstein 2012; Clarke 2013 and 2014a);
- Corporate governance is neglectful of diversity, creativity, and innovation in corporate forms and activity;
- Corporate governance is unaware of its impact upon the intensification of inequality in both the corporation and wider society (Ireland 2005; Piketty 2014; Clarke et al. 2019);
- Corporate governance is a discipline with a narrow focus on empirical studies of abstracted variables and bereft of attempts at holistic explanations of integrated and interrelated social and economic institutions and systems; and
- Corporate governance is ill-equipped to deal with the urgent imperative of climate change and to deliver sustainable enterprise.

The advance of corporate governance over the last century has proved highly contested as different eras of governance, with associated paradigms of explanation and implementation, have both reflected and reinforced changes in the wider political economy through successive eras of corporate governance (Figure 4). For much of the twentieth century, the lessons of world wars and the Great Depression of the 1930s had confirmed how essential it was to keep institutions and industry firmly grounded in the common interest of maintaining economic prosperity and social justice. Yet in the competitive economies pursuing expansion and transformation in the 1970s, there was a reawakening of sterner philosophies.

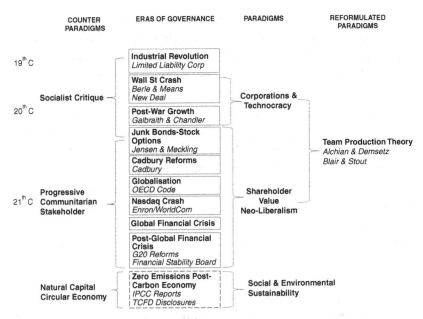

Figure 4 Evolution of Corporate Governance Paradigms

Towards the end of the twentieth century it seemed apparent that the market-based system, and the neoclassical economic rationale on which it was constructed, was very much in the ascendancy. Among the strongest intellectual forces of this neoclassical legacy is undoubtedly a particularly lethal, stripped-down interpretation of agency theory and shareholder value. How the crudest of conceptions could capture such a hegemonic hold in the way corporations are conceived is a subject worthy of deep study in the sociology of knowledge. The reformulation of team production theory by Margaret Blair and Lynn Stout (1999 and 2001; Clarke 2015a) presents a more recognizable and meaningful explanation of the purpose of the corporation and the duties of directors, though more radical critiques would suggest the imminent need for a recognition of the corporation as commons (Deakin 2019).

10.2 Changing Paradigms of Corporate Governance

Throughout the last century there were always radical voices that offered a different critique of the political economy of capitalism, and the role of large, multinational corporations that increasingly dominated the global economy. In different eras, socialist, progressive, communitarian, and stakeholder ideas possessed resonance, and an appeal to an alternative economic and political system, that led to many countries pursuing a different path of economic development. It should not be forgotten that for much of the twentieth century in many countries large sectors of industry were placed into public ownership because of the recognition of widespread market, governance, and managerial failure. While the international privatization movement since the 1980s Reagan/Thatcher era has reversed this trend, doubts remain about the viability of replacing public monopolies with private monopolies and oligopolies in many countries (Clarke & Pitelis 1995). In addition, the voluntary, social, and cooperative sectors of many economies remain large and vibrant, catering for needs the market neglects. Radical critiques of capitalism survive and have achieved a new resonance with the realization that unrestrained capitalism is threatening the ecology and community in a more critical way than ever before.

To meet the imminent challenge of social and environmental sustainability in a post-carbon economy, further rethinking of corporate purpose, corporate governance, and directors' duties will be essential (Clarke 2019a and 2020). This sustainability revolution has only just commenced, but in the course of the twenty-first century will transform business and society towards a digital, decentralized, and decarbonized future.

Presently there is a growing and insistent questioning of the sustainability of a carbon economy in the context of increasing pollution and global warming. While this interest in corporate social and environmental responsibility was deflected in the urgency of restoring financial stability following the global financial crisis, and more recently deflected by immediate concerns relating to the Covid-19 pandemic, it is these profound questions of the impact of corporations upon social and environmental sustainability that will preoccupy the paradigmatic contests of corporate governance throughout the remaining decades of the twenty-first century. In a context where the adequacy of the existing dominant paradigms of corporate governance is increasingly challenged, the search for coherent new paradigms is a vital task for corporate governance in the future.

References

ACGA. (2018) *Awakening Giant: The Evolution of Corporate Governance in China*, Hong Kong: Asian Corporate Governance Association

Adams, R. B., Almeida, H., and Ferreira, D. (2005) Powerful CEOs and Their Impact on Corporate Performance, *Review of Financial Studies* 18(4): 1403–32

Adams, R., Hermalin, B., and Weisbech, S. (2010) The Role of Boards of Directors in Corporate Governance, *Journal of Economic Literature*, 48, 58–107

Aglietta, M. and Rebérioux, A. (2005) *Corporate Governance Adrift: A Critique of Shareholder Value*, Cheltenham, Northampton MA: Edward Elgar

Aguilera, R. and Jackson, G. (2003) The Cross-national Diversity of Corporate Governance: Dimensions and Determinants, *Academy of Management Review*, 28(3): 447–65

Aguilera, R. V. and Cuervo-Cazurra, A. (2004) Codes of Good Governance Worldwide: What is the Trigger? Organization Studies, 25(3): 415–443

Aguilera, R. V. and Jackson, G. (2010) Comparative and International Corporate Governance, *Academy of Management Annals*, 4(1): 485–556

Aquilera, R. V., Florackis, C., and Kim, H. (2016) Advancing the Corporate Governance Research Agenda, *Corporate Governance: An International Review*, 24, 3, 172–80

Aguilera, R. V., Talaulicar, T., Chung, C., Jimenez, G., and Goel, S. (2016) Cross-National Perspectives on Ownership and Governance in Family Firms, *Corporate Governance: An International Review*, 2015, 23 (3) 161–6

Akerlof, G. and Shiller, R. J. (2009) *Animal Spirits: How Human Psychology Drives the Economy, and Why it Matters for Global Capitalism*, Princeton, NJ: Princeton University Press

Alchian, A. A. and Demsetz, H. (1972) Production, Information Costs and Economic Organisation, *American Economic Review*, 62, 777–95

Amable, B. (2003) *The Diversity of Modern Capitalism*, Oxford: Oxford University Press

Apreda, R. (2003) The Semantics of Corporate Governance: The Common Thread Running Through Corporate, Public, Global Governance, Working Paper Series 245, November, University of CEMA, Argentina

Araki, T. (2005) Corporate governance reforms, labour law developments, and the future of Japan's practice-dependent stakeholder model, *Japan Labor Review* 2(1): 26

Armitage, S., Hou. W., Sarkar, S., Talaulicar, T. (2017) Corporate Governance Challenges in Emerging Economies, *Corporate Governance: An International Review*, 25, 148–54

Arnold, B. and de Lange, P. (2004) Enron: An Examination of Agency Problems, *Critical Perspectives on Accounting*, 15. 751–765.

Bansal,P. and Hoffman, A. (2011) *The Oxford Handbook of Business and the Natural Environment*, Oxford University Press

Barker, S. Baker-Jones, M. Barton, E., and Fagan, E. (2016) Climate change and the fiduciary duties of pension fund trustees – lessons from the Australian law, *Journal of Sustainable Finance & Investment*, 6:3, 211–44

Barney, J. (1999) Firm Resources and Sustained Competitive Advantage, *Journal of Management*, 17, 99–120

Bauer, R. and Guenster, N. (2003) *Good Corporate Governance Pays Off: Well-Governed Companies Perform Better on the Stock Market*, Working Paper, University of Maastricht, April

Baumann, D. and Scherer, A. G. (2010) *MNEs and the UN Global Compact: An Empirical Analysis of the Organizational Implementation of Corporate Citizenship*, Institute of Organization and Administrative Science, University of Zurich, IOU Working Paper No. 114

Baysinger, B. and Hoskisson, R. (1990) The Composition of Boards of Directors and Strategic Control: Effects on Corporate Strategy, *Academy of Management Review* 15(1):72–87

Bebchuk, L. and Roe, M. (1999) A Theory of Path Dependence in Corporate Ownership and Governance, *Stanford Law Review*, 52: 775–808

Bebchuk, L. and Fried, J. (2005) Pay without Performance: Overview of the Issues, *Journal of Corporation Law*, 30 (4): 647–73

Bebchuk, L. A. and Jackson, R. J. (2005) Executive Pensions, *Journal of Corporation Law*, 30(4): 823–55

Benn, S. and Dunphy, D. (2007 *Corporate Governance and Sustainability*, London and New York: Routledge

Berle, A. A. and Means, G. C. (1933) *The Modern Corporation and Private Property*, Chicago: Commerce Clearing House

Berger, S. and Dore, R. (eds). 1996. *National Diversity And Global Capitalism*. Ithaca, NY: Cornell University Press

Bigley, G. A. and Wiersma, M. F. (2002) New CEOs and corporate strategic refocusing: How experience as heir apparent influences the use of power. *Administrative Science Quarterly*, 47, 707–727

Bird, A. (1990) Power and the Japanese CEO, *Asia Pacific Journal of Management* 7(2): 1–20

Blair, M. M. (1995) *Ownership and Control: Rethinking Corporate Governance for the 21st Century*, Washington DC: Brookings Institute

Blair, M. M. (1999) Firm-Specific Human Capital and Theories of the Firm, in M. M. Blair and M. J. Roe (eds), *Employees and Corporate Governance*, Brookings Institution Press

Blair, M. M. (2012) In the Best Interests of the Corporation: Directors' Duties in the Wake of the Global Financial Crisis, in T. Clarke and D. Branson (eds), *The Sage Handbook of Corporate Governance*, London: Sage, 62–80

Blair, M. M. and Roe, M.J (1999a) *Employees and Corporate Governance*, Washington: Brookings Institute

Blair, M. M. and Stout, L. A. (1999b) A Team Production Theory of Corporate Law, *Virginia Law Review*, 85(2): 247–328

Blair, M. and Stout, L. (2001) Director Accountability and the Mediating Role of the Corporate Board, *Washington University Law Quarterly*, 79: 403

Bogle, J. C. (2008) Corporate America to Its Owners: Owners of the World Unite!, in T. Clarke and M. dela Rama (eds), *Fundamentals of Corporate Governance: Volume 1 Ownership and Control*, London: Sage, 326–42

Boyer, R. and Drache D. (1996) *States against Markets: The Limits of Globalization*, London: Routledge

Boyer, R. (2005) From Shareholder Value to CEO Power: the Paradox of the 1990s, *Competition and Change* 9(1): 7

Bozec, R. (2005) Board of Directors, Market Discipline and Firm Performance, *Journal of Business Finance and Accounting*, 32 (9&10): 1921–60

Bratton, W. and Wachter, M. (2010) The Case Against Shareholder Empowerment, *University of Pennsylvania Law Review*, 653–728

Brennan, M. J. (2004) *How Did It Happen?* Anderson Graduate School of Management and Finance, Paper 4-04, University of California, Los Angeles

Buchanan, J., Chai, D., and Deakin, S. (2014) Agency Theory in Practice: A Qualitative Study of Hedge Fund Activism in Japan, *Corporate Governance: An International Review*, 2014, 22(4): 296–311

Business Roundtable (2019) Statement on the Purpose of a Corporation, Business Roundtable, Washington DC

Cadbury Report (1992) *Report of the Committee on the Financial Aspects of Corporate Governance*, London: Gee Publishing

Cadbury, A. (2000) Foreword, in *World Bank, Corporate Governance: A Framework for Implementation*, Washington, DC: World Bank

Cadbury, A. (2002) *Corporate Governance and Chairmanship*, Oxford: Oxford University Press

Cai, P. (2017) Understanding China's Belt and Road Initiative, Sydney: Lowy Institute, https://www.lowyinstitute.org/sites/default/files/documents/Understanding%20China%E2%80%99s%20Belt%20and%20Road%20Initiative_WEB_1.pdf

Calder, F. and Culverwell, M. (2005) *Following up the World Summit on Sustainable Development Commitments on Corporate Social Responsibility*, Royal Institute of International Affairs, London: Chatham House

Carney, M. (2008) Corporate Governance and Competitive Advantage in Family- Controlled Firms, in T. Clarke and M. dela Rama, *Fundamentals of Corporate Governance: Volume 1 Ownership and Control*, London: Sage, 247–63

Carter, C. C. and Lorsch, J. W. (2004) *Back to the Drawing Board: Designing Corporate Boards for a Complex World*, Boston, MA: Harvard Business School Press

Çelik, S. and Isaksson. M. (2014) Institutional Investors and Ownership Engagement, *OECD Financial Market Trends*, 2013/2

Cernat, L. (2004) The Emerging European Corporate Governance Model: Anglo-Saxon, Continental or Still the Century of Diversity? *Journal of European Public Policy*, 11 (1): 147–66

Certo, S. T., Lester, R. H., Dalton, C. M., and Dalton, D. R. (2006) Top Management Teams, Strategy and Financial Performance: A Meta-Analytic Examination, *Journal of Management Studies*, 43 (4): 813–39

Chandler, A. D. (1977) *The Visible Hand: The Managerial Revolution in American Business*, Cambridge, MA: Belknap Press

Christian Aid (2004) *Behind the Mask: The Real Face of Corporate Social Responsibility*, London: Christian Aid

Cioffi, J. W. (2000) Governing Globalization? The State, Law, and Structural Change in Corporate Governance. *Journal of Law and Society*, 27 (4): 572–600

Claessens, S., Djankov, S., and Lang, L. H. P. (2000) The Separation of Ownership and Control in East Asian Corporations, *Journal of Financial Economics*, 58(1): 81–112

Claessens, S. and Fan, J. (2002) Corporate Governance in Asia, *International Review of Finance*, *3*, 2, 71–103

Claessens, S. (2004) *Corporate Governance and Development*, Global Corporate Governance Forum, Washington DC: World Bank

Clarke, G. and Hebb, T. (2004) Pension Fund Corporate Engagement: The Fifth Stage of Capitalism, *Industrial Relations*, 59, 1, 142–71

Clarke, F. and Dean, G. (2007) *Indecent Disclosure: Gilding the Corporate Lily*, New York: Cambridge University Press

Clarke, T. (1978) Industrial Democracy: The Institutionalised Suppression of Industrial Conflict ?, in T. Clarke and L. Clements, *Trade Unions Under Capitalism*, London: Fontana, 351–82

Clarke, T. (1998) The Stakeholder Corporation: A Business Philosophy for the Information Age, *Long Range Planning – International Journal of Strategic Management*, Pergamon, 31(2): 182–94

Clarke, T. (2000) Haemorrhaging Tigers: The Power of International Financial Markets and the Weaknesses of Asian Modes of Corporate Governance, *Corporate Governance: An International Review*, 8(2): 101–16

Clarke, T. (2004a) *Theories of Corporate Governance: The Philosophical Foundations*, London and New York: Routledge

Clarke, T. (2004b) Cycles of Crisis and Regulation: The Enduring Agency and Stewardship Problems of Corporate Governance, *Corporate Governance: An International Review*, 12(2): 153–61

Clarke, T. (2005) *Corporate Governance: Critical Perspectives*, Five Volumes, London: Routledge

Clarke, T. (2007) The Evolution of Directors' Duties: Bridging the Divide between Corporate Governance and Corporate Social Responsibility, *Journal of General Management*, 32(3): 1–27

Clarke, T. (2009) A Critique of the Anglo-American Model of Corporate Governance, *Comparative Research in Law and Political Economy*, 5,3, 1–38

Clarke, T. (2010) Recurring Crises in Anglo-American Corporate Governance, *Contributions to Political Economy*, 29(1): 9–32

Clarke, T. (2013) Deconstructing the Mythology of Shareholder Value, *Accounting, Economics, and Law*, 3(1): 15–42

Clarke, T. (2014a) Dangerous Frontiers in Corporate Governance, *Journal of Management and Organization*, 20(3): 268–86

Clarke, T. (2014b) The Impact of Financialisation on International Corporate Governance, *Law and Financial Markets Review*, 8(1): 39–51

Clarke, T. (2014c) High Frequency Trading and Dark Pools: Sharks Never Sleep, *Law and Financial Markets Review*, December, 8, 4, 342–51

Clarke, T. (2015a) The Long Road to Reformulating the Understanding of Directors' Duties: Legalising Team Production Theory, *Seattle University Law Review*, 38: 433–87

Clarke, T. (2015b) Changing Paradigms in Corporate Governance: New Cycles and New Responsibilities, *Society and Business Review*, 10(3): 306–26

Clarke, T. (2016a) The Widening Scope of Director's Duties: The Increasing Impact of Corporate Social and Environmental Responsibility, *Seattle University Law Review*, 39: 557–602

Clarke, T. (2016b) The Continuing Diversity of Corporate Governance: Theories of Convergence and Diversity, *Ephemera*, 16(1): 19–52

Clarke, T. (2017) *International Corporate Governance: A Comparative Approach*, London and New York: Routledge Second Edition

Clarke, T. (2019a) The Greening of the Corporation, in Clarke, T., O'Brien, J. and O'Kelley, J. (2019) *The Oxford Handbook of the Corporation*, Oxford University Press, 589–640

Clarke, T. (2019b) Creative Destruction, Technology Disruption and Growth, *Oxford Research Encyclopedia of Economics and Finance*, OUP https://oxfordre.com/economics/view/10.1093/acrefore/9780190625979.001.0001/acrefore-9780190625979-e-393?rskey=sjHwKI

Clarke, T. (2020) The Contest on Corporate Purpose: Why Lynn Stout Was Right and Milton Friedman Was Wrong, *Accounting, Economics and Law – A Convivium*, 10, 3

Clarke, T and Boersma, M. (2017) The Governance of Global Value Chains: Unresolved Human Rights, Environmental and Ethical Dilemmas in the Apple Supply Chain in China, *Journal of Business Ethics*, Vol. 143, Issue 1, 111–31

Clarke, T and Boersma, M. (2019) Global Corporations and Global Value Chains: The Disaggregation of Corporations?, in Clarke, T., O'Brien, J. and O'Kelley, J. (2019) *The Oxford Handbook of the Corporation*, Oxford University Press, 319–65

Clarke, T. and Bostock, R. (1994) International Corporate Governance: Convergence and Diversity, in T. Clarke and E. Monkhouse, *Rethinking the Company*, London: Financial Times Pitman

Clarke, T. and Bostock, R. (1997) Governance in Germany: The Foundations of Corporate Structure? in: K. Keasey, S. Thompson, and M. Wright (eds). *Corporate Governance: Economic and Financial Issues*, Oxford, 233–51

Clarke, T. and Chanlat, J-F. (2009) *European Corporate Governances: Readings and Perspectives*, London: Routledge

Clarke, T. and dela Rama, M. (2006) *Corporate Governance and Globalisation*, London: Sage

Clarke, T., Gholamshahi S., and Jarvis, W. (2019) The Impact of Corporate Governance on Compounding Inequality: Maximising Shareholder Value and Inflating Executive Pay, *Critical Perspectives on Accounting*, 63, 1–17

Clarke, T. and Klettner, A. (2011) Corporate Governance and the Global Financial Crisis: The Regulatory Responses, in C. Ingley and A. Tourani-

Rad (eds), *Handbook of Emerging Issues in Corporate Governance*, World Scientific Publishing and Imperial College Press, 71–102

Clarke, T. and Lee, K. (2018) *Innovation in the Asia Pacific: From Manufacturing to the Knowledge Economy*, Singapore: Springer

Clarke, T. and Monkhouse, E. (1994) *Rethinking the Company*, London: Financial Times

Clarke, T. and Monkhouse, E. (1995) *Rependsando a Empresa*, Sao Paulo: Pioneira

Clarke, T., O'Brien, J., and O'Kelley, J. (2019) *The Oxford Handbook of the Corporation*, Oxford University Press

Clarke, T. and Pitelis, C. (1995) *The Political Economy of Privatisation*, London: Routledge

Clarke. T. and Pitelis, C. (2005) *The Political Economy of Privatisation*, London: Routledge

Clearfield, A. M. (2005) With Friends Like These, Who Needs Enemies? The Structure of the Investment Industry and Its Reluctance to Exercise Governance Oversight, *Corporate Governance: An International Review*, 13(2): 114–21

Coase, R. (1937) The Nature of the Firm, *Economica*, 4

Coffee, J. C. (1991) Liquidity versus Control: The Institutional Investor as Corporate Monitor, *Columbia Law Review* 91(6): 1329–68

Coffee, J. (2000) Convergence and Its Critics: What Are the Preconditions to the Separation of Ownership and Control? Columbia Law School, Center for Law and Economic Studies, Working Paper No. 179

Coffee, J. (2002) Convergence and Its Critics: What are the Preconditions to the Separation of Ownership and Control? in J. A. McCahery, P. Moerland, T. Raaijmakers and L. Renneboog (eds), *Corporate Governance Regimes: Convergence and Diversity*, Oxford: Oxford University Press

Cogan, D. G. (2006) *Corporate Governance and Climate Change: Making the Connection.* Boston, MA, CERES

Coles, J. W. and Hesterly, W. (2000) Independence of the Chairman and Board Composition: Firm Choices and Shareholder Value, *Journal of Management* 26(2): 195–214

Colli, A. and Colpan, A. (2016) Business Groups and Corporate Governance: Review, Synthesis, and Extension, *Corporate Governance: An International Review*, 2016, 24(3): 274–302

Conyon, M. (2006) Executive Compensation and Reward, *Academy of Management Perspectives*, 20, 1,25–44

Conyon, M. J. and Peck, S. I. (1998) Board Control, Remuneration Committees, and Top Management Compensation, *The Academy of Management Journal*, 41(2): 146–57

Corporate Responsibility Coalition (2005) *Corporate Social Responsibility in the Finance Sector in Europe*, London: Corporate Responsibility Coalition (CORE)

Crane, A., Matten, D., and Spence, L. J. (2014a) *Corporate Social Responsibility: Readings and Cases in a Global Context*, London: Routledge

Crane, A., Palazzo, G., Matten, D., and Spence, L. J. (2014b) Contesting the Value of 'Creating Shared Value', *California Management Review*, 56(2):130–49; 151–3

Cuomo, F, Mallin, C., and Zattoni, A. (2016) Corporate Governance Codes: A Review and Research Agenda, *Corporate Governance: An International Review*, 24 (3) 222–41

Daily, C. M., Dalton, D. R., and Cannella, A. C. (2003) Corporate Governance: Decades of Dialogue and Data, *Academy of Management Review*, 28(3): 371–82

Das, S. (2011) *Extreme Money: The Masters of the Universe and the Cult of Risk*, Harlow: Portfolio

Datta, D. K., Guthrie, J. P., and Rajagopalan, N. (2002) Different industries, different CEOs? A study of CEO career specialization. *Human Resource Planning*, 25(2), 14–25

David, P., Bloom, M., and Hillman, A. J. (2007) Investor Activism, Managerial Responsiveness and Corporate Social Performance, *Strategic Management Journal*, 28: 91–100

Davis, E. P. and Steil, B. (2001) *Institutional Investments*, MIT Press: Cambridge, MA

Davis, G. (2005) New Directions in Corporate Governance, *Annual Review of Sociology*, Vol. 31, 143–62, August 2005

Davis, E. P. (2008) Institutional Investors, Corporate Governance and the Performance of the Corporate Sector, in T. Clarke and M. dela Rama, *Fundamentals of Corporate Governance: Volume 1 Ownership and Control*, London: Sage, 276–300

Davis, J. H., Schoorman, F. D., and Donaldson, L. (1997) Toward a Stewardship Theory of Management, *The Academy of Management Review*, 22(1): 20–47

Davis, S., Lukomnik, J and Pitt-Watson, D. (2006) *The New Capitalists: How Citizen Investors are Reshaping the Corporate Agenda*, Boston, MA: Harvard Business School Press

Deakin, S. (2005) The Coming Transformation of Shareholder Value, *Corporate Governance An International Review*, 13, 1, 11–18

Deakin, S. (2019) The Evolution of Corporate Form: From Shareholder's Property to Corporation as Commons, in T.Clarke et al., *The Handbook of the Corporation*, Oxford University Press, 687–710

Deeg, R. and Jackson, R. (2007) Towards a More Dynamic Theory of Capitalist Variety, *Socio-Economic Review*, 5(1): 149–79

Demb, A. and Neubauer, F. F. (1992) *The Corporate Board: Confronting the Paradoxes*, New York: Oxford University Press

Demsetz, H. and Lehn, K. (1985) The Structure of Corporate Ownership: Causes and Consequences, *Journal of Political Economy* 93: 1155–1177

Doane, D. (2005) The Myth of CSR, *Stanford Social Innovation Review*, Stanford University Graduate School of Business, Fall: 23–9

Dore, R. (2000) *Stock Market Capitalism: Welfare Capitalism*, Oxford, New York: Oxford University Press

Dore, R. (2002) Will Global Capitalism Be Anglo-Saxon Capitalism? *Asian Business & Management*, 1(1): 9–18

Drobetz, W., Schillhofer, A., and Zimmerman, H. (2004) Corporate Governance and Expected Stock Returns: Evidence from Germany, *European Financial Management*, 10(2): 267–293

Durisin, B. and Puzone, F. 2009. Maturation of corporate governance research, 1993–2007: An assessment, *Corporate Governance: An International Review*, 17: 266–91

Edwards, M., Kelly, S., Klettner, A., and Brown, P. (2019) *Unlocking Australia's Sustainable Finance Potential*. University of Technology Sydney

EIU (2008a) *Corporate Citizenship: Profiting from a Sustainable Business*, Economist Intelligence Unit, http://graphics.eiu.com/upload/Corporate_Citizens .pdf

Elhagrasey, G. M., Harrison, J. R., Bucholz, R, (1998) Power and Pay: The Politics of CEO Compensation, *Journal of Management and Governance* 2(4): 311–34

Enrione, A., Mazza, C., and Zerboni, F. (2005) Institutionalizing Codes of Governance, *New Public and Private Models of Management*, Skagen 27 May 2005, http://citeseerx.ist.psu.edu/viewdoc/download?doi=10.1.1 .1029.1314&rep=rep1&type=pdf

Epstein, M. J. and Roy, M. J. (2005) Evaluating and monitoring CEO performance: evidence from US compensation committee reports, *Corporate Governance*, Emerald 5 (4): 75–87

European Commission (2014a) Commission Working Document Executive Summary of the Impact Assessment SWD (2014) 126 Final Accompanying Document Directive 2007/36/EC Encouragement of Long Terms Shareholder Engagement Com (2014) 213 Final

European Commission (2014b) *Corporate Social Responsibility, National Public Policies in the European Union*, European Union

European Commission (2016) Council Directive on a Common Corporate Tax Base, European Commission

European Commission (2016) *Council Directive: Laying Down Rules Against Tax Avoidance Practices*, European Commission

Faccio, M. and Lang, L. (2008) The Ultimate Ownership of Western European Corporations, in T. Clarke and M. dela Rama, *Fundamentals of Corporate Governance: Volume 1 Ownership and Control*, London: Sage, 199–228

Fama, E. (1980) Agency Problems and the Theory of the Firm, *Journal of Political Economy*, 88, 2, 288–307

Fama, E. F. and Jensen, M .C. (1983) *Separation of Ownership and Control*, Journal of Law and Economics, 26, 301–26

Fernandez, C. and Arrondo, R. (2005) Alternative Internal Controls as Substitutes of the Board of Directors, *Corporate Governance – An International Review*, 13, 6, 856–66

Filatotchev I. and Wright M. (2017) Methodological issues in governance research: An editor's perspective, *Corporate Governance: An International Review*, 25:454–60

Financial Stability Oversight Council (FSOC) (2013) *Annual Report*, Washington, DC

Financial Times (2005) US Downturn, 17 November 2005

Fleckenstein, F. (2008) *Greenspan's Bubbles: The Age of Ignorance at the Federal Reserve*, New York: McGraw Hill

Fortune (2018) *Global 500*, Fortune, http://fortune.com/global500/

Frentrop, P. M. L. (2003) *A History of Corporate Governance 1602–2002*, Brussels: Deminor

Frentrop, P. (2019) The Dutch East India Company, in T.Clarke, J.O'Brien and C. O'Kelley (2019) *The Oxford Handbook of the Corporation*, Oxford University Press, 51–74

Frey, B. S. and Osterloh, M. (2005) Yes, Managers Should Be Paid Like Bureaucrats, *Journal of Management Inquiry* 14 (1): 96–111

G20 (2009) *Enhancing Sound Regulation and Strengthening Transparency*, G20 Working Group

G20/OECD (2015) *Principles of Corporate Governance*, Paris: OECD

Gadhoum, Y., Lang, L., and Young, L. (2008) Who Controls US? in T. Clarke and M. dela Rama, *Fundamentals of Corporate Governance: Volume 1 Ownership and Control*, London: Sage, 148–70

Galbraith, J. K. (1967) *The New Industrial State*, New York: New American Library

Garriga, M. and Melé, D. (2004) Corporate Social Responsibility Theories: Mapping the Territory, *Journal of Business Ethics*, 53: 51–71

Gelter, M. (2009) The Dark Side of Shareholder Value, *Harvard International Law Journal*, 50, 1, 129–94

Georgakakis D. and Ruigrok,W. (2017) CEO Succession Origin and Firm Performance, *Journal of Management Studies*, 54(1) 58–87

Gereffi, G. and Sturgeon, T. (2013) Global Value Chains and Industrial Policy: The Role of Emerging Economies, in D. Elms and P. Low (eds), *Global Value Chains in a Changing World*, Geneva: World Trade Organization, Fung Global Institute, Temasek Foundation Centre for Trade and Negotiations, 329–60

Global Reporting Initiative (GRI) (2011a) *Sustainability Reporting Guidelines*, Version 3.1, GRI.

Global Reporting Initiative (GRI) (2011b) *GRI and ISO 2600: How to Use the GRI Guidelines in Conjunction with ISO 26000*, GRI

Global Reporting Initiative (GRI) (2015) *Defining Materiality: What Matters to Reporters and Investors*, Global Reporting Initiative

Global Reporting Initiative (GRI) (2015a) *GRI's History*, GRI

Godden, L., Rochford, F., Peel, J., Caripis, L., and Carter, R. (2013) Law, Governance and Risk: Deconstructing the Public-Private Divide in Climate Change Adaptation, *UNSW Law Journal*, Vol 61, 1, 224–55

Gompers, P., Ishii, J., and Metrick, A. (2003) *Corporate Governance and Equity Prices*, The Quarterly Journal of Economics, 118, 1

Goobey, A. R. (2005) Developments in Remuneration Policy, *Journal of Applied Corporate Finance* 17: 36–40

Goodijk, R. (2000) Corporate Governance and Workers Participation, *Corporate Governance* 8: 303–10

Goyer, M. (2001) Corporate Governance and the Innovation System in France, *Industry and Innovation*, 8 (2): 135–58

Grandori, A. (2006) *Corporate Governance and Firm Organization: Micro-foundations and Structural Forms*, Oxford: Oxford University Press

Grossman, S. and Hart, O. (1980) Takeover Bids and the Free-Rider Problem and the Theory of the Corporation, *Bell Journal of Economics*, 11, 42–64

Gugler, K. (Ed) (2001) *Corporate Governance and Economic Performance*, Oxford: Oxford University Press

Hall, P. and Soskice, D. (2001) *Varieties of Capitalism: The Institutional Foundations of Comparative Advantage*, New York: Oxford University Press

Hamilton, D. and Quinlan, J. (2005) *Deep Integration: How Transatlantic Markets Are Leading Globalisation*

Hansmann, H. and Kraakerman, R. (2001) The End of History for Corporate Law, *Georgetown Law Review*, 89: 439

Harris, C. (2003) *Private Participation in Infrastructure in Developing Countries*, World Bank Working Paper No. 5, World Bank

Hart, O. (1983) The Market Mechanism as an Incentive Scheme, *Bell Journal of Economics*, 1983, 14, 2, 366–382

Hawken, P., Lovins, A. B., and Lovins, L. H. (1999) *Natural Capitalism: The Next Industrial Revolution*, London: Earthscan

Hawley, J. and Williams, A. (2008) The Emergence of Universal Owners: Some Implications of Institutional Equity Ownership, T. Clarke and M. dela Rama, *Fundamentals of Corporate Governance: Volume 1 Ownership and Control*, London: Sage, 264–75

Held, D. and McGrew A. (2002b) *Governing Globalization – Power, Authority and Global Governance*, Cambridge: Polity Press

Helm, D. (2015) *Natural Capital: Valuing the Planet*, New Haven and London: Yale University Press

Henwood, D. (1998) *Wall St.*, London/New York, NY: Verso

Hernandez, M. (2008) Promoting Stewardship Behavior in Organizations: A Leadership Model, *Journal of Business Ethics* (2008) 80: 121–8

Hernandez, M. (2012) Toward and Understanding of the Psychology of Stewardship, *Academy of Management Review*, Vol. 37, No. 2, 172–93

Hillman, A. J., Cannella, A. A., and Paetzold, R. L. (2000) The resource dependence role of corporate directors: strategic adaptation of board composition in response to environmental change, *Journal of Management Studies*, 37: 235–54

Hillman, A., Withers, M., and Collins, B. (2009) Resource Dependence Theory: A Review, *Journal of Management*, 20, 10, 1–24

Hirst, P. and Thompson, G. (1996) *Globalisation in Question: The International Economy and the Possibility of Governance*, Cambridge: Polity Press

Hollingsworth, J. R., Schmitter, P. C., and Streeck, W. (1994) Capitalism, Sectors, Institutions and Performance, in J. R. Hollingsworth, P. C. Schmitter, and W. Streeck (eds), *Governing Capitalist Economies*, Oxford University Press, New York, 3–16

Hoskisson, R. E. and Hitt, M. A. (1988) Strategic Control Systems and Relative R & D Investment in Large Multiproduct Firms, *Strategic Management Journal*, 9, 577–90

Huse, M. (2007) *Boards, Governance and Value Creation: The Human Side of Corporate Governance*, Cambridge University Press

Huse, M. and Gabrielsson, J. (2012) Board Leadership and Value Creation: An Extended Team Production Approach, in T. Clarke and D. Branson (eds), *The Sage Handbook of Corporate Governance*, London: Sage, 233–52

Huse, M. (2018) *Value-Creating Boards*, Cambridge Elements in Corporate Governance, Cambridge University Press

IFC (2015) *A Guide to Corporate Governance in the European Union*, Washington: International Finance Corporation

IPCC (2014) *Climate Change 2014: Impacts, Adaptation, and Vulnerability, Working Group II, Intergovernmental Panel on Climate Change*, vii

Ireland, P. (2005) Shareholder Primacy and the Distribution of Wealth, *Modern Law Review*, 68(1): 49–81

ISO 26000 (2010) *Guidance Standard on Social Responsibility*

Jacoby, S. M. (2004) *The Embedded Corporation: Corporate Governance and Employment Relations in Japan and the US*, Princeton: Princeton University Press

Jain, T. and Jamali, D (2016) Looking Inside the Black Box: The Effect of Corporate Governance on Corporate Social Responsibility, *Corporate Governance: An International Review*, 24 (3) 253–73

Jensen, M. C. and Meckling, W. H. (1976) Theory of the Firm: Managerial Behaviour, agency Costs, and Ownership Structure, *Journal of Financial Economics*, 3, 305–60

Jensen, M. C. (1986) Agency Costs of Free Cash Flow, Corporate Finance, and Takeovers, *The American Economic Review*, 76,2, 323–9

Kang, D. and Sorensen, A. (2008) Ownership Organisation and Firm Performance, T. Clarke and M. dela Rama, *Fundamentals of Corporate Governance: Volume 1 Ownership and Control*, London: Sage, 128–47

Kaufman, A. and Englander, E. J. (2005) A Team Production Model of Corporate Governance, *Academy of Management Executive*, 19(3): 9–22

Klettner, A., Clarke, T., and Boersma, M. (2014) Strategic and Regulatory Approaches to Increasing Women in Leadership: Multi-level Targets and Mandatory Quotas as Levers for Cultural Change, *Journal of Business Ethics*, 2016, 133 (3), 395–419

Kobrin, S. J. (2002) Economic Governance in an Electronically Networked Global Economy, in R. H. Bruce and T. J. Biersteker, *The Emergence of Private Authority in Global Governance*, New York: Cambridge University Press

Kumar, P. and Zattoni, A. (2015a), In Search of a Greater Pluralism of Theories and Methods in Governance Research, *Corporate Governance: An International Review*, 2015, 23(1): 1–2

Kumar, P. and Zattoni, A. (2015b) Ownership Structure, Corporate Governance and Firm Performance, *Corporate Governance: An International Review*, 23 (6) 469–71

Kumar, P. and Zattoni, A. (2016a) Family Business, Corporate Governance, and Firm Performance, *Corporate Governance: An International Review*, 24(6): 550–1

Kumar, P. and Zattoni, A. (2016b) Executive Compensation, Board Functioning, and Corporate Governance, *Corporate Governance: An International Review*, 24(1): 2–4

Lane, C. (2003) Changes in Corporate Governance of German Corporations: Convergence to the Anglo-American Model? *Competition and Change*, 7(2): 79–100

Lane, C. (2004) Globalization and the German model of capitalism – erosion or survival? *British Journal of Sociology*, 51 (2): 207–34

La Porta, R., Lopez-de-Silanes, F., and Shleifer, A. (1999) Corporate Ownership around the World, *Journal of Finance*, 54, 471–518

Lazonick, W. (2007) The US Stock Market and the Governance of Innovative Enterprise, *Industrial and Corporate Change*, 16, 3

Lazonick, W. (2010) The Chandlerian Corporation and the Theory of the Innovative Enterprise, *Industrial and Corporate Change*, 19, 2, 317–49

Lazonick, W. (2012) In the Name of Shareholder Value, in T. Clarke and D. Branson (eds), *The Sage Handbook of Corporate Governance*, London: Sage, 476–95

Lazonick, W. (2017) *Innovative enterprise solves the agency problem: the theory of the firm, financial flows, and economic performance*, Institute for New Economic Thinking, Working Paper No. 62

Learmont, S. (2002a) *Corporate Governance: What Can Be Learned from Japan?* Oxford: Oxford University Press

Lindgreen, A. and Swaen, V. (2010) Corporate Social Responsibility, *International Journal of Management Reviews*, 12(1): 1–7

Loring, J. M. and Taylor, C. K. (2006) Shareholder Activism: Directional Responses to Investors' Attempts to Change the Corporate Governance Landscape, *Wake Forest Law Review* 41(1): 321

Lorsch, J. and MacIver, E. (1989) *Pawns or Potentates: The Reality of America's Corporate Boards*, Boston, MA: Harvard Business School Press

Lorsch, J. W., Berlowitz, L., and Zelleke, A. (2005) *Restoring Trust in American Business*, Cambridge, Massachusetts: MIT Press

MacAvoy, P. W. and Millstein, I. M. (2004) *The Recurrent Crisis In Corporate Governance*, Stanford Business Books

Mace, M. L. (1971) *Directors: Myth and Reality*, Boston, MA: Harvard University Press.

Mason, A, D. and Shetty, S. (2019) *A Resurgent East Asia: Navigating a Changing World*. World Bank East Asia and Pacific Regional Report;. Washington, DC: World Bank

Matolcsy, Z., Stokes, D., and Wright, A. (2004) Do independent directors add value, *Australian Accounting Review* 14 (1): 33–40

Matsumura, E. and Shin, J. (2005) Corporate Governance Reform and CEO Compensation: Intended and Unintended Consequences, *Journal of Business Ethics* 62: 101–13

McCahery, J. A., Moerland, P., Raaijmakers, T., and Renneboog, L. (2002) *Corporate Governance Regimes: Convergence and Diversity*, Oxford: Oxford University Press

McDonnell, B. (2002) Convergence in Corporate Governance: Possible But Not Desirable, *Villanova Law Review* 341, 350–3

McDonough, W. J. (2005) Corporate Board Elections and Internal Controls, 27 September, Federal Reserve Bank of New York

McKinsey and Company (2008) *Mapping Global Capital Markets, Fourth Annual Report*, San Francisco, CA: McKinsey Global Institute

McNulty, T. and Nordberg, D. (2016)Ownership, Activism and Engagement: Institutional Investors as Active Owners, *Corporate Governance: An International Review*, 24(3): 346–58

Michels, R. (2001) *Political Parties: A Sociological Study of Oligarchical Tendencies of Modern Democracy*, Kitchener: Batoche Books

Mills, C. W. (1971) *The Power Elite*, NewYork: Oxford University Press

Mitchell, L. A. (2001) *Corporate Irresponsibility: America's Newest Export*, New Haven, CT: Yale University Press

Mizruchi, M. S. (1983) Who controls whom? An examination of the relation between management and boards of directors in large American corporations, *Academy of Management Review* 8(3): 426–35

Moerland, P. W. (1995) Alternative Disciplinary Mechanisms in Different Corporate Governance Systems, *Journal of Economic Behaviour and Organisation*, 26, 17–34

Nelson, J. (2014) Corporate Social Responsibility: Emerging Good Practice for a New Era, OECD Observer

Neubaum, D. O. and. Zahra, S. (2006) Institutional Ownership and Corporate Social Performance: The Moderating Effects of Investment Horizon, Activism, and Coordination, *Journal of Management*, 32(1): 108–31

O'Brien, J. (2014) Culture Wars: Rate Manipulation, Institutional Corruption, and the Lost Normative Foundations of Market Conduct Regulation, *Seattle University Law Review*, 37: 375–83

O'Connor, M. (2000) Labor's Role in the American Corporate Governance Structure. *Comparative Labor Law & Policy Journal* 22: 97–134

Ocasio, W. (1994) Political dynamics and the circulation of power: CEO succession in US industrial corporations 1960-1990, *Administrative Science Quarterly* 39: 285–312

OECD Business Sector Advisory Group (1998) *Corporate Governance: Improving Competitiveness and Access to Global Capital Markets*, Paris: OECD

OECD (1996) *Globalisation of Industry – Overview and Sector Reports*, Paris: OECD

OECD (2001) *New Patterns of Industrial Globalisation: Cross-Border Mergers and Acquisitions and Strategic Alliances*, Paris: OECD

OECD, (2004) *Corporate Governance: A Survey of OECD Countries*, Paris: OECD

OECD (2005) *Measuring Globalisation: OECD Economic Globalisation Indicators*, Paris: OECD

OECD Watch (2005) *Five Years On: A Review of the OECD Guidelines and National Contact Points*, Amsterdam: Centre for Research on Multinational Corporations.

OECD (2008) *Guidelines for Multinational Enterprises*, Paris: OECD

OECD (2009) *Annual Report on the OECD Guidelines for Multinational Enterprises 2008*, Paris: OECD

OECD (2012) *Mapping Global Value Chains*, Paris: Working Party of the Trade Committee, Paris: OECD

OECD, WTO, and UNCTAD (2013) *Implications of Global Value Chains for Trade, Investment, Development and Jobs*, Report to G20. Paris: Organization for Economic Cooperation and Development

OECD (2017a) *OECD Survey of Corporate Governance Frameworks in Asia*, Paris: OECD

OECD (2017b) *Methodology for Assessing the Implementation of the G20/ OECD Principles of Corporate Governance*, Paris: OECD

OECD (2018a) *Annual Report on the OECD Guidelines for Multinational Enterprises 2018*, Paris: OECD

OECD (2018b) *Flexibility and Proportionality in Corporate Governance*, Paris: OECD

OECD (2019) *Corporate Governance Factbook 2019*, Paris: OECD

O'Sullivan, M. A. (2001) *Contests for Corporate Control: Corporate Governance and Economic Performance in the United States and Germany*, London: Oxford University Press

Pareto, V. (1991) *The Rise and Fall of Elites: An Application of theoretical sociology*, Transaction Publishers: New Brunswick, NJ

Petrella, R. (1996) Globalization and internationalization: the dynamics of the emerging world order, in, R. Boyer and D. Drache, *States Against Markets*, Routledge, pp. 62–84

Phillips, K. (2008) *Bad Money: Reckless Finance, Failed Politics and the Global Crisis of American Capitalism*, London: Penguin

Piketty, T. (2014) *Capital in the 21st Century*, Cambridge, MA: Belknap Press

Polanyi, K. (1957) *The Great Transformation: The Political and Economic Origins of Our Time*, Boston, MA: Beacon Press

Post, J. E. (2002) *Redefining the Corporation: Stakeholder Management and Organizational Wealth*, Stanford, CA.: Stanford Business Books

Pugliese, A. and Zattoni, A. (2012) Board's Contribution to Strategy and Innovation, in T. Clarke and D. Branson (eds), *The Sage Handbook of Corporate Governance*, London: Sage, 217–32

PWC (2020) *Asset Management 2020 A Brave New World*, PWC

RIAA (2015) *Driving Long Term Investment and Delivering Responsible Financial Markets: A Preliminary Paper on Industrial Priorities*, Sydney: Responsible Investment Association of Australasia

Roberts, J., McNulty, T., and Stiles, P. (2005) Beyond Agency Conceptions of the Work of the Non-Executive Director: Creating Accountability in the Boardroom, *British Journal of Management* 16: S5–S26

Ruigrok,W., Peck, S., Tacheva, S., Greve, P., and Hu, Y. (2006) The Determinants and Effects of Board Nomination Committees, *Journal of Management and Governance* 10(2): 119–48

Ryan, L. and Dennis, B. (2003) The Ethical Undercurrents of Pension Fund Management, *Business Ethics Quarterly*, 13(3), 313–335

Ryan, L. V. and Schneider, M. (2008) The Antecedents of Institutional Investor Activism, in T. Clarke and M. dela Rama, *Fundamentals of Corporate Governance: Volume 1 Ownership and Control*, London: Sage, 301–25

Schembera, S. (2012) *Implementing Corporate Social Responsibility: Empirical Insights on the Impact and Accountability of the UN Global Compact*, Business Working Paper Series, Working Paper No. 316, University of Zurich

Schiehll, E. and Martins, H. C. (2016) Cross-National Governance Research: A Systematic Review and Research Assessment, *Corporate Governance: An International Review*, 24 (3), 181–99

Schumpeter, J. A. (1939) *Business Cycles*, New York: McGraw Hill

Searcy, C. (2012) Corporate Sustainability Performance Measurement Systems: A Review and Research Agenda, *Journal of Business Ethics*, 107: 239–53

Seki, T. (2005) Legal Reform and Shareholder Activism by Institutional Investors in Japan, *Corporate Governance: An International Review*, 13(3): 377–85

Seki, T. (2019) The Japanese Corporation: Community, Purpose and Strategy, in, T.Clarke, J. O'Brien, and C. O'Kelley, *The Oxford Handbook of the Corporation*, OUP, 418–456

Seki, T. and Clarke, T. (2014) The Evolution of Corporate Governance in Japan: The Continuing Relevance of Berle and Means, *Seattle University Law Review*, 37: 717–47

Selznick, P. (1957) *Leadership in Administration*, Evanston, IL: Row, Peterson

Shleifer, A. and Vishny, R. W. (1986) Large Shareholders and Corporate Control, *Journal of Political Economy*, 94: 461–88

Shleifer, A. and Vishny, R. W. (1997) A Survey of Corporate Governance, *The Journal of Finance*, LII (2) 737–83

Simon, H. A. (1991) Organizations and Markets, *Journal of Economic Perspectives*, 5, 25–44

Smith, A (2006) *The Theory of Moral Sentiments*, Dover Books, Minuela, NY (originally published 1759)

Smith, A. (1976) *An Inquiry into the Nature and Causes of the Wealth of Nations*, Chicago, IL: University of Chicago Press (originally published 1776)

Spira, L. F. (1999) Ceremonies of Governance: Perspectives on the Role of the Audit Committee, *Journal of Management and Governance* 3: 231–60

Stathopoulos, K. and Voulgaris, G. (2016) The Importance of Shareholder Activism: The Case of Say-on-Pay, *Corporate Governance: An International Review*, 2016, 24(3): 359–70

Stern, N. (2006) *Stern Review: The Economics of Climate Change*

Stern, P. J. (2019) English East India Company-State and the Modern Corporation, in T. Clarke, J. O'Brien and C. O'Kelley (2019) *The Oxford Handbook of the Corporation*, Oxford University Press, 75–92

Stiglitz, J. (2002) *Globalization and Its Discontents*, London: Allen Lane Penguin Press

Stiglitz, J. (2008) Realign Wall Street's Interests, *Harper's Magazine*, November, 36–37

Stiles, P. and Taylor, B. (2002) *Boards at Work*, Oxford University Press

Stout, L. (2012) *The Shareholder Value Myth*, San Francisco, CA: Berrett-Koehler

Stout, L. (2019) Corporations as Sempiternal Legal Persons, in T. Clarke, J. O'Brien, and C. O'Kelley (eds), *The Oxford Handbook of the Corporation*, Oxford University Press, 220–33

Sullivan, R. and Mackenzie, C. (2006) *Responsible Investment*, Sheffield: Greenleaf Publishing

Sundaramurthy, C. and Lewis, M. (2003) Control and Collaboration: Paradoxes of Governance, *Academy of Management Review*, 28(3): 397–415

Takeshi, I. (2001) From Industrial Relations to Investor Relations? Persistence and Change in Japanese Corporate Governance, Employment Practices and Industrial Relations, *Social Science Japan Journal* 4: 225–41

Taylor, B. (2003) Corporate Governance: The Crisis, Investors' Losses, and the Decline in Public Trust, *Corporate Governance: An International Review*, 11(3): 155–63

Teece, D. and Pitelis, C. (2009) The (new) nature and essence of the firm, *European Management Review*, 6, 5–15

Tricker, R. (2008) The Ideology of Corporate Governance, in T. Clarke and M. dela Rama, *Fundamentals of Corporate Governance, Volume 1 Ownership and Control*, London: Sage, 1–9

Turley, S. and Zaman, M. (2004) The Corporate Governance Effects of Audit Committees, *Journal of Management & Governance* 8(3): 305–32

Turnbull, S. (2012) The Limitations of Corporate Governance Best Practices, in T. Clarke and D. Branson (eds), *The Sage Handbook of Corporate Governance*, London: Sage, 428–50

UNCTAD (2002) Trans National Corporations and Export Competitiveness, World Investment Report, Geneva: United Nations Conference on Trade and Development

UNEP (2019) *Emissions Gap Report 2019*, United Nations Environment Programme

UN Global Compact (UNGC)/Global Reporting Initiative (GRI) (2007) *Making the Connection: The GRI Guidelines and the Global Compact Communication on Progress*, GRI

UNEP Finance Initiative (2018) Rethinking Impact to Finance the SDGs, UNEP Finance Initiative

Useem, M. and Mitchell, O. S. (2000) Holders of the Purse Strings: Governance and Performance of Public Retirement Systems, *Social Science Quarterly*, 81 (2): 489–506

Useem, M. (2012) The Ascent of Shareholder Monitoring and Strategic Partnering: The Dual Functions of the Corporate Board, in T. Clarke and D. Branson (eds), *The Sage Handbook of Corporate Governance*, London: Sage, 136–58

van Essen, M., Strike,V., Carney, M., and Sapp, S. (2015) The Resilient Family Firm: Stakeholder Outcomes and Institutional Effects, *Corporate Governance: An International Review*, 2015, 23(3): 167–83

Veldman, J. (2019) Inequality Inc, *Critical Perspectives on Accounting*, 16

Veltrop, D. B., Molleman, E., Hooghiemstra R., and van Ees, H. (2017) Who's the Boss at the Top? A Micro-Level Analysis of Director Expertise, Status and Conformity Within Boards, *Journal of Management Studies*, 54 (7) 1079–1110

Vera-Muñoz, S. C. (2005) Corporate Governance Reforms: Redefined Expectations of Audit Committee Responsibilities and Effectiveness, *Journal of Business Ethics* 62(2): 115–27

Vogel, D. (2005) *The Market for Virtue: The Potential and Limits of Corporate Social Responsibility*, Washington, DC: Brookings Institute

Wang, H. and Barney, J. (2006) Employee Incentives to Make Firm-Specific Investments, *Academy of Management Review*, 3, 12, 466–76

Warren, E. (2017) *21st Century Glass-Steagall Act*, Washington: US Senate

Weir,C., Laing, D., and McKnight, P. (2008) Internal and External Governance Mechanisms: Their Impact on the Performance of Large UK Public Companies, in T. Clarke and M. dela Rama, *Fundamentals of Corporate Governance: Volume 2 Boards and Directors*, London: Sage, 14–36

Weinstein, O. (2012) Firm, Property and Governance: From Berle and Means to the Agency Theory, and Beyond. *Accounting, Economics and Law: A Convivium*, 2(2)

Whitehouse, L. (2006) *Corporate Social Responsibility: Views from the Frontline*, Journal of Business Ethics, 63: 279–96

Whyte, M. K. (1996) The Chinese Family and Economic Development: Obstacle or Engine? *Economic Development and Cultural Change*, 45, 1, 1–30

Williamson, O. E. (1975) *Markets and Hierarchies: Analysis and Anti-Trust Implications*, New York: Free Press

Williamson, O. E. (1985) *The Economic Institutions of Capitalism*, New York: Free Press.

Wood, R. E. (2004) How Independent is your compensation committee? *Benefits Law Journal* 17 (4): 82–97

World Bank (1993), *The East Asian Miracle: Economic Growth and Public Policy*, Oxford University Press, Washington, DC

World Bank (2006) *Making Global Value Chains Work for Development*, World Bank

World Bank (2016) The world's top 100 economies: 31 countries; 69 corporations, People, Spaces, *Deliberation*, The World Bank blog

World Bank (2018) *Riding the Wave: An East Asian Miracle for the 21st Century*, World Bank East Asia and Pacific Regional Report;. Washington, DC: World Bank

World Business Council for Sustainable Development (WBCSD) (2014) *Changing Pace*, www.wbcsd.org/Pages/EDocument/EDocumentDetails .aspx

World Business Council for Sustainable Development (WBCSD) (2015) *The CEO Guide to Climate Action 2015*

World Business Council for Sustainable Development (WBCSD) (2020). *Toward Common Metrics and Consistent Reporting of Sustainable Value Creation*, World Economic Forum

World Economic Forum (2012) *Emerging Best Pratices of Chinese Globalizers: The Corporate Global Citizenship Challenge*, World Economic Forum

World Economic Forum (2013), From the Margins to the Mainstream Assessment of the Impact Investment Sector and Opportunities to Engage Mainstream Investors, World Economic Forum http://www3.weforum.org /docs/WEF_II_FromMarginsMainstream_Report_2013.pdf

World Economic Forum (2014) *Towards the Circular Economy: Accelerating the Scale-Up across Global Supply Chains*

World Economic Forum (2018) *Sustainable Development Impact Summit*, World Economic Forum

World Economic Forum, (2018a) Annual Impact Investor Survey, World Economic Forum

World Economic Forum (2020) *How Social and Environmental Responsibility Can Boost Business*, World Economic Forum

World Federation of Stock Exchanges (2018) *Market Statistics December 2018*, London: World Federation of Stock Exchanges

World Federation of Exchanges (2019) Market Highlights, World Federation of Exchanges

Wright, C. and Nyberg, D. (2015) Climate Change, Capitalism and Corporations: Processes of Creative Self-Destruction, Cambridge: Cambridge University Press

Yoshikawa, T. (2018) *Asian Corporate Governance*, Cambridge Elements in Corporate Governance, Cambridge University Press

Yuan, W., Bao, Y., and Verbeke, A. (2011) Integrating CSR Initiatives in Business: An Organizing Framework, *Journal of Business Ethics*, 101: 75–92

Zattoni, A. (2011) Who should control a corporation? Towards a contingency stakeholder theory for allocating ownership rights, *Journal of Business Ethics*, 103: 255–74

Zattoni, A. and Van Ees, H. (2012) How to contribute to the development of a global understanding of corporate governance? Reflections from submitted and published articles in CGIR. *Corporate Governance: An International Review*, 20, 106–18

Zattoni, A. and Pugliese, A. (2012) Board's Contribution to Strategy and Innovation, in T. Clarke and D. Branson (eds), *The Sage Handbook of Corporate Governance*, London: Sage, 217–31

Zeitlin, M. (2008) Corporate Ownership and Control: The Large Corporations and the Capitalist Class, in T. Clarke and M. dela Rama, *Fundamentals of Corporate Governance: Volume 1 Ownership and Control*, London: Sage, 90–127

Corporate Governance

Thomas Clarke
UTS Business School, University of Technology Sydney

Thomas Clarke is Professor of Corporate Governance at the UTS Business School of the University of Technology Sydney. His work focuses on the institutional diversity of corporate governance and his most recent book is *International Corporate Governance* (Second Edition 2017). He is interested in questions about the purposes of the corporation, and the convergence of the concerns of corporate governance and corporate sustainability.

About the series

The series Elements in Corporate Governance focuses on the significant emerging field of corporate governance. Authoritative, lively, and compelling analyses include expert surveys of the foundations of the discipline, original insights into controversial debates, frontier developments, and masterclasses on key issues. Its areas of interest include empirical studies of corporate governance in practice, regional institutional diversity, emerging fields, key problems, and core theoretical perspectives.

Cambridge Elements ⁼

Corporate Governance

Elements in the series

A full series listing is available at: www.cambridge.org/ECG